GUERRILLA WARFARE

by 'Yank' Levy

PENGUIN BOOKS, INC.

THE INFANTRY JOURNAL, INC.

NEW YORK   WASHINGTON

Publishers Note—THIS BOOK IS PUBLISHED JOINTLY BY PENGUIN BOOKS, INC., 245 FIFTH AVE., NEW YORK, AND THE INFANTRY JOURNAL, INC., WASHINGTON, D. C.

Illustrations by Corporal James A. Ernst

First printed March, 1942
Second printing April, 1942
Third printing June, 1942
Fourth printing September, 1942
Fifth printing December, 1942

PRINTED IN THE U. S. A. BY H. WOLFF, NEW YORK

THE AUTHOR

Bert Levy was born in Hamilton, Ontario, of mixed Canadian stock on October 5th, 1897. When he was three months old his parents moved to the United States. and he grew up in Cleveland, Ohio. He had the normal education of an American worker, including some years of night High School, but when asked about his education he answers: "My real education was in the school of hard knocks."

He was a deck hand or stoker in the Merchant Service in 1916 and early 1917; he returned to seafaring in 1939 and early 1940. When there are no submarines about, the sea does not interest him.

He served in the 39th Battalion, Royal Fusiliers, during 1918-19, in Palestine and Trans-Jordan. His own notes then read: "Mexico, 1920-1, and some gun-running; Nicaragua, 1926"; and there are other entries. He served in the International Brigade in Spain, joining early in 1937, and becoming an officer in the machine-gun company of the British Battalion. He was captured on the Jarama and spent six months in General Franco's prisons.

He joined the Staff of the Osterley Park School for the Home Guard in August, 1940, and has been lecturing to the Home Guard at the War Office No. 1 School and elsewhere for the past 15 months.

PREFACE

MILITARY authorities in the great armies of the world have looked upon guerrilla warfare, until very recent years, as merely a troublesome mode of fighting that might be encountered in wild and isolated regions. There was little conception of it as an organized method of war that millions of civilized citizens might use in defending their homelands against direct attack. And this despite the example of the Boers early in this century.

Now, however, no doubt can be left of the value of guerrilla methods. They are important, not only to organized armies, but even more to the auxiliary units of citizens known in Great Britain as Home Guards and generally in our country as State Guards. Indeed, guerrilla warfare offers to volunteer local units more promise of effective action against invading forces than standard tactics. For the battle methods of small military units are chiefly based on the closest cooperation with other combat units, and not on independent fighting. Squads, platoons, and companies of an army fight in the main with like units close by them, and with powerful supporting units backing them up with all kinds of weapons from machine guns to artillery and bombers—the whole directed by a higher commander. Such units must know independent guerrilla methods, too. But the chances are high that most of their fighting will be done as part of a close-knit, larger force.

It is true, as Bert Levy clearly implies in this book, that a home-defense unit will also act under orders of a higher commander, cooperating within its own region with other such bodies and with the regular forces posted there. (In Britain, the Home Guards form an integral part of the Army.) But owing to their regional distribution such units must chiefly prepare to operate independently and without immediate support.

In this country, many State Guard units and other locally formed groups have been seeking practical detailed information on methods of warfare they can use in their training. Knowing that Home Guards in Britain and guerrilla-trained groups in China, Russia, the Philippines, and in occupied countries have developed sound methods of harassment and resistance, they have wanted to know more about these methods. They have wanted to go beyond mere drill, first-aid, and other basic training, to the adaptation of guerrilla war to their own local problems of defense.

The Army itself has also taken the closest interest in guerrilla developments in view of their large-scale use by other armies. And it is clearly recognized that Army training in such methods is a part of training for modern war.

To American home-defense units, however, the fighting methods of Great Britain's Home Guards have especial interest. For the British units have gone through many months of development and training toward meeting a continuously expected invasion. Their problems have been closely similar to those our own home-defense units have more recently been facing. And they have become a great, nationwide force of local groups, recognized officially and officially aided.

The author of this book, Bert Levy, is a Home Guard instructor experienced in guerrilla fighting methods. His descriptions of these methods have much of value for the local forces of America. As he presents them they are of course fitted to British town and country. But most of what he says can readily be applied to our own American scene. Some of the methods the author gives are very similar to those now included in military texts. But some are new, many of them embody fresh applications of old methods, and only a few may not fit our own ideas of fighting.

My indorsement of *Guerrilla Warfare* is naturally a personal rather than an official one. But I look upon it as a description of practical ways of small-unit fighting viewed by the author with the utmost realism. We of this country who may conceivably become engaged anywhere with the enemy should study and, it may be, apply these ways of war. Not even a seeming remoteness of encounter can stand for a moment as an excuse for unreadiness.

LT. COL. JOSEPH I. GREENE

U. S. ARMY

Editor, *The Infantry Journal*

Washington, February, 1942.

INTRODUCTION

MANY thousands, perhaps hundreds of thousands, of the Home Guard know my friend "Yank" Levy. For those who have heard him, at the Osterley Park Training School for the Home Guard, at the first War Office School for Instructors of the Home Guard, or at the lectures he has been giving from one end of the country to another, "Yank" needs no introduction. This Canadian is without question the best lecturer—most convincing, most detailed and most practical—on the tactics of guerrilla warfare available in Britain.

But many of those who have heard him, and others to whom this booklet will come, may not have realized the basis of experience from which he talks and writes. As soon as he was old enough to handle a weapon he was, to use his own words, "mixed up in Mexico." He fought in the last Great War, in Palestine and in the desert beyond Jordan. He has taken part in some of the little "troubles" that have occasionally occurred south of Mexico; I shall not be more specific about these troubles, because I gather that a thirty years' sentence for gun-running still makes him occasionally pensive. He served with the International Brigade in Spain as an officer, and a very good one, in the battalion which I commanded. He was captured south of Madrid

7

and spent about six months in General Franco's prisons. Released by an exchange of prisoners, he had to be restrained by his friends from returning to Spain, and wrote to me from Canada a little later with the request that I should use my influence to get him a passport, so that he could come back to Spain. He volunteered to join the Canadian Army as soon as this war broke out, and was turned down for flat feet or hammer toes—or perhaps, more seriously, for his reputation as one of the most obstreperous leaders of Canada's unemployed.

But "Yank" was not going to be kept out of it. At a time when our war had not really started, early in 1940, he worked his passage over here as one of the "black gang," a stoker on a tramp steamer. Finding that there was no interesting fighting to get into, he continued to work at this job, possibly because it was the most dangerous he could then find. One of his ships went down a week after he left it. He left it to find some sort of war job in Britain. After trying such a job he came to help me at Osterley, and has been teaching the Home Guard ever since. He is still looking for a more interesting and exciting thing to do; any offers sent to him, care of the publisher of this book, will be given due consideration.

So much for the man. Now for the subject on which he writes. I believe guerrilla warfare to be an absolutely vital element in any formula for our victory.

"Yank" is a practical man and not a theoretician. Guerrilla warfare is a very practical business. But some of those who read this may have in their minds objections of a theoretical sort, doubts about the effectiveness of guerrilla warfare under modern conditions. Some soldiers trained on text-books of the past or influenced—quite correctly—by the convincing theorists of mechanized warfare, and by the even more convincing Nazi achievements in mechanized warfare, may think of guerrilla warfare as something of secondary and minor importance, something that cannot "really count now." And because there are such persons, soldiers and civilians, it may be useful for me to give a little of the theory of the thing.

Those who believe that the tank is the dominant arm in modern warfare are correct. Those who see in the plane, and particularly in the dive-bomber, the decisive supporting arm that must be linked closely with the tank—are also correct. As a matter of fact, and not of theory, these weapons used in masses have secured decision in enough campaigns to establish the Nazi power from Madrid to near Moscow. But because these things are so, because these facts have happened, because these campaigns have been won, we dare not say that it will always be so, that campaigns will always be won mainly by these weapons, that there is no chance of ever defeating a superior force of tanks and planes. To do so would be to consider Nazi methods of warfare the final unchangeable top limit in the development of the art of war. It would be to neglect the fact that war is always changing and can always be changed. And I believe that the direction in which war is changing today can be seen in fact and action, can be understood and further developed. That direction, as I see it, is towards the combination between the methods and tactics of mechanized warfare and those of guerrilla warfare.

There are many reasons for this belief of mine. One is that the Red armies of the Soviet Union have for months been resisting, without disaster, the forces of almost all Europe, organized with German thoroughness and flung into battle with Nazi disregard for loss. Their way of resistance has clearly proved effective and dangerous to Hitler's armies. And part of the method of the Red armies of the Soviet Union has been the use of the tactics of guerrilla warfare, not only by peasant snipers and bands of civilians turned guerrillas, but also by units, large or small, of Russian infantry surrounded by or passed by the swift manœuvres of German armoured and unarmoured vehicles.

Another reason for my belief is more theoretical. Mechanized military force has an armored spearhead very hard to check or destroy. It backs that spearhead with masses of planes and with infantry and artillery whose fire-power protects them against most weapons. But this formidable combination has behind it a weak point: it needs more supplies than any previous type of armed force, and these supplies cannot normally be brought close to the armoured spearhead by railway, but must be spread over a network of roads and carried mainly by relatively unprotected convoys of lorries.

It is the communications of an armoured force, the roads and the lorry-convoys that it needs, that are most vulnerable. But they are not easily vulnerable to our normal infantry and artillery. They are vulnerable to two types of force: our own defending armoured force, with aeroplane support, and our guerrillas.

Those who rightly say that we must make tanks and planes, in vast quantities, sometimes wrongly think that these machines should be opposed directly, head-on, to the enemy machines of similar types. Tank should hunt tank, they think, and plane should shoot down plane. Which is like trying to use a pair of nutcrackers to put out of action another pair of nutcrackers. Nutcrackers should be used against nuts. Our air-tank combat teams should be used against the most sensitive, most vulnerable, parts of the enemy's forces. Blitz needs to be answered by counter-blitz. But it is not possible for any defending force continually to exert this type of pressure against an attacker. The guerrilla, on the other hand, can exert against the communications of any enemy force, against his dumps as well as his lorries, his headquarters as well as his stragglers, a continual pressure, a threat that wears out men and forces. And guerrilla warfare is a method of fighting—a useful method, that will, I believe, in future campaigns become absolutely essential to success—that can be achieved and developed by democracies and by socialist societies, but cannot be developed by Fascism, particularly in the areas where Fascism rules by force against the will of the population.

Successful guerrilla fighting needs the self-confidence

10

and initiative of millions of free men, the support at risk and at heavy sacrifice of almost all the population, and a feeling of close comradeship and solidarity between the guerrilla troops and any regular army and air force supporting them. The Nazis cannot get these qualities at their service, in any of the occupied countries of Europe, even in Italy. We can. And therefore we should not think of guerrilla warfare only in terms of the present heroism of the Soviet Union, or a possible future resistance to invasion in this country. We should think of it also in terms of our own invasion of the Continent. We should be looking for ways of fighting, and combinations between ways of fighting, that can enable a democratic force invading Hitler's Europe to mobilize and use the enormous power of the "hundred million allies" who can be ours.

"Yank" Levy and myself, with others who helped us at Osterley and elsewhere, have been preaching the principles of guerrilla warfare, and teaching its practical details, since June, 1940. We did not learn these principles and details from Crete; and we have been rather amused since the fighting in Crete to find things advocated officially as "lessons of Crete" that we had been advocating nine months before as lessons of common sense.

Fully three-quarters of this book had been written before June, 1941, when the Nazis attacked Russia and guerrilla war came into the newspapers in a big way. The book was delayed because I had to work on another, a book on mechanized warfare. It was not until this study of "official" war was out of the way that I could turn to the "unofficial" type of warfare described here.

The book on mechanized warfare, on the Nazis' tactics and the reply to them (*Blitzkrieg*, by F. O. Miksche), answers those friends and critics who have protested that we who are advocates of guerrilla war give too much importance to this form of warfare.

We are not advocates of guerrilla warfare as opposed to, or in contrast to, mechanized warfare. We are advocates of a combination between the two, in defense and in attack.

We have been advocating this combination of two very different methods of fighting since the formation of the Home Guard. And I do not understand those who say that our only way to win this war is by making more tanks and more planes than the Nazis can make. The Nazis have a start in the arms race; it is by no means clear that our production in 1941, even with America's help, was enough to reduce that start. It seems quite possible that, at the moment when I write this, Nazi Europe is making more tanks and planes than are being made by Britain and America. And while we try to catch up on the Nazis, or try to wake up enough to begin to overhaul them, the Nazi armies conquer new territories. They gain new sources for steel, for other metals out of which to make planes and tanks. I do not see where this process ends, or that it necessarily has an end that is pleasant to contemplate. It seems to me that those who rely solely on this race to pile up materials are pessimists, and blind to the main hope that we can have now and in the future. That main hope is, to put it in another way, the hope that men can still beat machines, that materialist simple addition of tank to tank and plane to plane is not the measuring rod of warfare, that today as in the past Napoleon's words hold true: "the moral is to the physical in war as three to one."

Guerrilla warfare is warfare against the enemy's morale and his material. It hits at morale where morale is weakest, behind the picked units and the men securely armoured. It hits at material when that material is not in a state to hit back. In a later chapter, for which I am partly responsible, this book tells some of the past of guerrilla warfare. There have been "invincible" armies in the past. There have been the legions of Rome and the proud chivalry of the Middle Ages. And at the same time there have been forces despised by all professional soldiers, barbarians with battle-axes or churls with long-bows, who have met and destroyed utterly the proudest and most heavily armoured "modern" armies of their day. This is something that can happen again. I may be optimistic to believe that it can happen soon, next year. But I believe it is happening now, on a limited scale, spontaneously, almost inevitably. If we can make the process conscious, if we can understand what is happening to us, and join our understanding and our will-power to press it forward and improve it, then I believe that this war can be won far more quickly than by any other way. That is why I recommend this book not only to every member of the Home Guard but to every soldier who understands that we may need to do a little thinking for victory, and to every civilian who wants to understand what is happening and can happen in this war, how to help if invasion comes to this country, how the Nazis are going to be defeated.

TOM WINTRINGHAM

Surrey, November, 1941.

CHAPTER I

HISTORY never repeats itself. But there are many things which some of us thought belonged wholly to the past which recur, from time to time, throughout the centuries, in somewhat different form, and brought about by different circumstances. Guerrilla warfare is one of those things.

There are some who have thought and said, "Guerrilla fighting is a thing of the past, or at least it belongs only to bits of warfare in distant places, in which backward peoples are involved—on the north-west frontier of India, for example." But these people are thinking still—as, unfortunately, so many still do—in the terms of the World War of 1914 to 1918, of a war with firmly locked, extensive "fronts."

Modern warfare—not only the present great war, but the Civil War in Spain and the war now raging in China—has brought back guerrilla fighting, for now there are no fixed, rigid, long-term "fronts."

Moreover, the dividing line between guerrilla warfare and other forms of what we may call "irregular warfare" has become less distinct; and, from the storehouse of guerrilla tactics, methods and ruses, the regular soldier, and, still more the Home Guard, may gather invaluable aid. This book, while designed primarily to inform those of us who may be involved in real guerrilla fighting, contains also, I hope, much to interest the professional soldier and also the member of Britain's human bulwark against invasion: the Home Guard.

It was after lecturing for nearly a year on the subject of guerrilla warfare, its methods and tactics, that it occurred to me that there was no single handbook—so far as I know -- devoted solely to this art. There are books which deal incidentally with guerrilla warfare, and numerous excellent books on woodcraft, stalking, scouting, and other matters which, while part of guerrilla warfare, are also in use in regular warfare. Quite often my listeners have asked me to make it possible for them to have in written form some of the material I have given them in speech or demonstration. So that, although not much of a hand at writing, I have constructed this small book for them and for others who may be interested.

First of all, let us consider just what is guerrilla warfare. The word is Spanish, its literal meaning "little war," from the Spanish word *Guerra*, "War." The Spanish dictionary which I have carried around with me for many years in South America and Spain says: "Guerrilla: War of partisans." In other words, not war as carried on by regular soldiers, but by people who are partisans of one side or another, of one cause or another. And the term "partisan warfare" is sometimes used instead of "guerrilla"—notably in descriptions of the Russian Revolutionary Wars and the Chinese-Japanese War. But, remember, guerrilla warfare is not directed against other guerrillas, but against regulars.

Guerrilla warfare is that method of fighting which is employed by men living in an area occupied or surrounded by the enemy. That is as good a definition as any. I some-

14

times like to term it "wasp warfare," for that expresses
something of the harassing, irritating, sting-and-run kind
of fighting which guerrilla warriors must employ. "Must
employ," I say, because, in comparison with the enemy's
army of regulars, guerrilla forces are likely to be small, in-
sufficiently armed at best, without permanent bases or sure
sources of supply, and in constant danger.

On the other hand, the enemy is strong, organized, in
control of supplies and key positions—in that portion of
territory which he has managed to grasp. Let us suppose
that some particular corner of England, Wales or Scotland
(or Ireland too, for that matter, although the Irish are kind
of slow to realize it) has been cut off by enemy forces which
have managed to make a successful landing; these forces
are consolidating their control over this area, before advancing further into our country. Outside the occupied
corner lie our regular forces, blasting at the enemy from
without. But we—partisan troops, regulars detached from
their units, Home Guards, anybody who wants to serve,
and is capable of serving, as a guerrilla fighter—have organized our bands within the enemy territory. While our
troops are penning them in from outside, and preparing
to advance and drive them back into the sea, it is our job to
buzz around the enemy, stabbing him here, then there,
with sudden unexpected jabs, destroying or appropriating
his stores, munitions and supplies, cutting his communications, trapping his messengers, ambushing his convoys or
lorries. In general, creating a considerable amount of hell,
and wearing him down.

Just a word here regarding the Home Guard. They are
not a guerrilla force in the strict sense of the term. They
are "irregulars"—somewhere half-way between regulars
and guerrillas.

But to draw this distinction becomes increasingly difficult in modern warfare which is so essentially fluid, mobile.
In the present fighting between Germany and the Soviet
Union, for example, Russian regular formations have
sometimes been by-passed by a German advance, and they

15

then immediately adopt guerrilla tactics, harrying the enemy in the rear, attacking his transport and communications, and so on.

But before we go any further let me stress one point: a guerrilla force can operate successfully only in an area in which the civilian population is not merely passively in sympathy with them, but in which there is a fair proportion who will give them active and willing assistance. From the civilian population, the guerrillas obtain supplies and information, and even recruits for their bands, as we shall see in further chapters.

I have said above that it is becoming increasingly difficult to draw a sharp distinction between guerrilla and other forces. The labels—regulars, irregulars and guerrillas—now apply more to the original methods of recruitment, the organization and equipment of these forces; less and less do such distinguishing terms apply to *methods of fighting*, against the swiftly fluctuating background of modern war.

In fact, I think we might go further and say that most of modern warfare may be defined as a kind of development and "regularization" of guerrilla warfare, or, if you prefer it, regular warfare into which substantial elements of guerrilla warfare have been injected.

A brief examination of the methods employed by the Germans in war will at once reveal how true is the above conclusion. The basic principle of German technique, both in strategy and tactics, appears to be to outflank the enemy, to disorganize his rear, in order, as far as possible, to avoid anything in the nature of old-fashioned pitched battle. The German Panzer divisions like steel-tipped fingers probe the enemy's lines, seeking for weak points. Once they find this weak point, they suddenly concentrate their strength against it for a surprise break-through. Once they have broken through, they dash ahead, by-passing the enemy's centres of resistance, avoiding direct combat with them, seeking always to drive through to the enemy's rear, as far and as fast as possible.

16

Surprise is an important factor in German technique. Each tank unit tries to appear suddenly and unexpectedly at some place in the rear, to spread disorganization and panic. And then to go on—always aiming for the weak spots and skirting the strong ones. After the tanks come the ordinary troops, mopping up the centres of resistance which the tanks have avoided, or, at least, tried to avoid—of course, they can't all get through. The follow-up troops also first attack the weakest resistance centres, first subduing them and then turning to the stronger ones. Always they attempt to take these strong points from the flank or rear.

Add to this the disorganization behind the lines caused by parachute or other air-borne troops, and the efforts of Fifth Columnists to add still further to the confusion and demoralization of the enemy.

And don't forget that all this activity is closely coordinated with the work of the air force, which is busy on reconnaissance work, dive-bombing troops, convoys or trains, battering at enemy aerodromes, and endeavouring to destroy his fighters and bombers in the air.

There are no longer any "fronts" in the old, rigid sense. In fact, one of the reasons for the swift successes of the German armies in France, Belgium and Holland was because the Germans just wouldn't settle down to the old conception of the linear front, while most of the generals on the other side refused to abandon that conception and insisted on trying to play the game their own old-fashioned way.

The whole process of the modern German technique may be likened to the spraying of blotting-paper with hundreds of drops of ink—the blotting-paper being the defended terrain, and the ink the attacking groups of the enemy. If you sprinkle enough drops on the blotter, they will begin to spread and merge, one with the other, until the whole sheet is covered. The thick line on the war-map, purporting to show you the "front," is nowadays misleading—for, in that sense, there is no front. Especially if both sides are using the new tactics, you will see that things are so mixed up that everybody seems to be on the flank or rear

17

of everybody else. Fighting can take place most anywhere, with troops fronting in any direction. To the inexpert onlooker it seems to be a glorious mix-up, a confused conglomeration of numerous deadly but small actions. But to the commanders—if they know their business and their communications are still working—there is a plan to it all, and they can co-ordinate the whole show.

Small actions, continual mobility, emphasis on rear or flanking attacks—these are all features of war in which the guerrilla fighter finds himself at home, far more so than if you were to plant him down for a month's dreary, if risky, residence in a mud-trench, as would have been the case in the last World War.

And now a further point of resemblance between modern regular warfare and guerrilla fighting. While, throughout the last couple of hundred years, armies have grown larger and larger, at the same time they have become more and more subdivided until now the smallest unit may be anything between three and ten men. The actual fighting has become a vast series of scraps between thousands of these small units. The guerrilla unit is almost always small, or it could not hide and operate. Moreover, this subdivision makes for individual resourcefulness and ability to command—also essential factors in guerrilla warfare.

In earlier wars it was only guerrilla forces which appeared way back in enemy territory, spreading panic and confusion. Now it may be air-borne troops or sudden tank and mechanized forays. To this extent the blitzkrieg technique may be termed a development of guerrilla warfare.

But we in Britain can go much farther than can the Germans, when it comes to the development and utilization of guerrilla methods, both for attack and defense. There are ways open to us which are closed to the Nazis. For we are men of democratic tradition, fighting for freedom, and guerrilla warfare is essentially the weapon of free men—a guerrilla band functioning efficiently under compulsion is inconceivable. Fascism or Nazism—and they are fundamentally the same—set out to destroy in men the very quali-

18

ties which are most prized in guerrilla fighting. Free men, hating oppression, with freedom of initiative and arms in their hands—these make the ideal guerrillas.

Therefore in the democratic countries there is far larger scope for the development of regular warfare along lines derived from guerrilla warfare. There are new ways of war which in this country and in Europe we can adopt, if we will—ways of war which the Nazis cannot and dare not use. We have already begun this process with the formation of the Home Guard. This is our answer to the German technique of attack and invasion. There is now no corner of Great Britain without its Home Guard unit. We have no rear—our defenses cover the whole country. There is nowhere—provided our organization is thorough and alert —where the Germans can appear unexpectedly. Even in the smallest village there are men who are armed and prepared. Let us see to it that their training and arming are adequate to meet the tactics which we know the Germans will employ.

A proper training in guerrilla methods will enable the Home Guard to deal swiftly and in deadly fashion with Germans dropped from parachutes or landed from troop-carrying planes and gliders, with marauding tanks or with Fifth Columnists. If they are properly trained, Home Guard units will know how to go on fighting even when cut off for days from other Home Guard or regular forces.

But when Britain launches her offensive in Europe, can you imagine the Nazis fighting in this manner, with an organization similar to our Home Guard, in France, Czechoslovakia or Norway, for instance—with the great majority of the civilian population against them, longing for their defeat?

And, even within Germany itself, it is doubtful whether the Germans could develop a force which would come anywhere near to our own Home Guard, in initiative, mobility and daring. Their fighting elite, you will suggest? Their Black Guards, or even the Storm Troopers? But don't forget that thousands of these in Germany—apart from the

19

thousands holding down the people in occupied countries —will be kept too busy keeping tab on other Germans who hate Nazism and long for deliverance from its rule, and who would actively assist us once they were convinced that our victory would give them freedom to fashion their own life and government independently. They dare not arm the whole population.

The importance to us of guerrilla fighting by rebels against Nazi rule, in any projected offensive on the Continent of Europe, is enormous and vital. It requires considerable modification of the strategy and tactics of our regular forces so that they may co-ordinate their efforts with those of the guerrilla forces. And here strategy and tactics link up with propaganda, which is, after all, an integral part of strategy, although the fact is not yet sufficiently recognized. So important is this subject that I have given some words to it at the end of this book.

The reader will note that, in the course of this book, I frequently address myself to the Home Guard, particularly when dealing with the preparatory knowledge—of territory, local inhabitants, etc.—which is so invaluable later, when guerrilla warfare is put into practice. I do this for two reasons: first, the Home Guard is particularly well qualified to carry on guerrilla warfare, in the event of an invasion and martial occupation of our territory, because of its knowledge of the local countryside, towns, villages, and so on; and, second, because—to tell the truth—I am so accustomed, from long experience of helping Home Guards with lectures and demonstrations, to dealing with men of this organization, that they come first to my mind.

But there is every reason why others should also learn the principles of guerrilla warfare, and apply them, if occasion arises. Everything in this book is designed for the information and use of every Britisher. Guerrillas can be recruited from any and all ranks and occupations. Particularly useful are Rover Scouts, hikers, gamekeepers—and don't let us forget those useful fellows; the poachers. For once gamekeepers and poachers can be united in the pursuit of a quarry—namely, the enemies of their country—whose destruction will benefit both.

In the chapters on practical guerrilla fighting, I deal with guerrilla warfare in what I might call its pure state—showing how men (and women too, for that matter) can fight even when isolated militarily, way within enemy-controlled territory. In other words, I state the extreme case, to give as clear a conception as possible of guerrilla methods. But there is nothing here which cannot be adopted, and adapted, under other circumstances, by partisans, Home Guards or regulars. The essence of guerrilla methods is their flexibility, the ease with which tactics may be modified and varied to suit any situation that may arise. Therefore, I offer these various practices, procedures and stratagems, not as blue-print plans to be followed slavishly and without imagination, but to be varied, combined or developed in accordance with the necessities of action.

CHAPTER II

ENGLAND had been conquered. The heavily armoured forces of the enemy, more mobile and equipped with better weapons than the defending forces, had broken every element of resistance throughout the country. Then in the fens and marshes of East Anglia an outlaw raised rebellion. He did not try to make an army that could stand against the overwhelming force of the enemy. He raised guerrilla bands to harry them. These bands hid in the marshes and stormed out from them to take towns as large as Peterborough.

That is not a gloomy description of something that might happen. It is a description of something that did happen, nearly 900 years ago. The armoured enemy was the army of King William the Conqueror. It was a force the English could not resist successfully in open battle, because its hitting power and mobility came from its kernel of armoured knights on horseback. The English at that time had no such "Panzer" force. The outlaw who raised rebellion against the Conqueror was Hereward the Wake. Accounts vary as to the length of his campaign, but it is likely that he held out for more than a year.

Just as men think today of ditches and lakes and marshes linked to protect their islands of resistance against tanks, so these guerrillas of 900 years ago made a stronghold in the Fens at Ely to which no armoured man and no horseman could penetrate. Only the light-footed, who knew where to tread and where to leap, could get across the barriers. King William's great qualities as a military leader were never better shown than in his drive against these "rebels"—"rebels" who in modern terms were fighting for a national cause against aggression. The historian of the period, John Richard Green, writes: "Nowhere had William found so stubborn a resistance: but a causeway two miles long was at last driven across the marshes, and the last hopes of English freedom died in the surrender of Ely."

Guerrillas do not always win. Why should they? No other form of fighting always wins. In this chapter about the history of guerrilla warfare it is worth while mentioning Hereward's lost campaign, because he might have won if there had been others like him, because the Conqueror might have been conquered if throughout Britain there had been men who knew how to use arms in a new way—in a way that did not pile men together to be slaughtered by the Norman knights but spread them out to harry and weary the invaders and destroy their supplies.

Naturally Hereward the Wake was not the first guerrilla leader. There were plenty before him: raiding Danes and Vandals and Goths and Huns—all the unpleasant people whose names are still used for hateful enemies. Many of those who worried and harassed the Legions of Rome, and wore them out until the Roman Empire broke, fought not as formed armies but as roving bands. But we have no need to go to that far past to find plenty of examples of effective guerrilla work.

Welsh, Scotch and Irish have all shown us such examples near home. The Welsh armies that kept the English busy, building castles and chasing up what the Welsh call mountains, for some hundreds of years, were often almost guerrilla forces. And because the Welsh could not afford the approved armour and weapons of the day, they improvized their own weapons and gradually made them better than similar things had been in the past. The Welsh invented the long-bow. Bows and arrows had been used for a long time in war, but nothing as powerful as this long-bow had ever been seen before. An unfortunate English knight was riding home, 750 years ago, after assembling a few Welsh villagers and kicking them in the pond, when a sniper bobbed up from behind a bush. The sniper's arrow went through the skirt of the mailed shirt that the knight was wearing—links of iron chain woven together. Then it went through his mailed breeches, then through his leg, then through his saddle which had a wooden board within it, and finally the point of the arrow stuck into the horse. As nasty a warning to the man on horseback as a certain type of grenade is going to be to the man in a tank.

The Welsh also specialized, it is clear from the war correspondents of those days, in what the Chinese guerrillas call "the short attack." One of these war correspondents, Giraldus Cambrensis, remarked that they risked everything on the result of one tempestuous charge; in five minutes they were either victorious or legging it hard up the mountain, where the armoured cavalry could not get at them.

After the Welsh, the Scots. Under King Robert the Bruce they fought an immensely successful guerrilla warfare, after most of their country had been conquered by the English King Edward. "Without any pitched battle, but by a long series of sieges, raids, and adventurous assaults on castles, Bruce had by 1314 cleared the English out of the whole land," says one of the history books. And how he did it was laid down in what the Scots called "gude King Robert's testiment." In these verses his troops were advised to fight "by hyll and mosse" (morass). They should have woods for their "wallis" (walls): that is, they should not try to fortify themselves behind walls, but should make their keeps and strong points in the forests. They should keep their stores "in strait placis" (in places hard to get at). And they should go in for the scorched earth tactic, and burn the plains: they should "byrnen ye planeland thaim before."

King Robert advised his soldiers to raid at night: "with wyles and waykings of the night and mekill noyis maid on hytht." Even in those days guerrilla fighters recognized that they must sometimes steal up quietly, and sometimes make a helluva noise up the hill to distract the enemy's attention.

There was not much real guerrilla fighting later on when the English were settling their little argument about Kings and Parliaments. But one aspect of guerrilla fighting occurred on both sides: people held out in castles or big houses or towns even when the armies of the other side were all round them. In each campaign it was the battle that mattered, and usually Cromwell won the battle. But he had seldom an easy job of it, and often a determining factor must have been the fact that some of the King's men were absent surrounding and "containing" islands of resistance held by the Parliament. In the Parliament's own area Cromwell mopped up similar islands of resistance by using artillery to batter down the walls. Although as I have said this was not exactly guerrilla warfare, it has this importance for us: that battles are decisive, but that odd bits of scrapping round the place can determine how great a force comes to battle on each side, and therefore which side wins the battle.

The Red Indians of North Africa defended their country against the pale-face invader by guerrilla tactics. These Red Indians were of course savages, but they also happen to be the inventors of modern warfare. They gave the British forces sent against them such an unpleasant time that those British forces had to unlearn a great many things, and learn many new things before they could be much use. Stiff English units all trained to move like clockwork soldiers on parade were always running into Indian ambushes. In one of the worst of these ambushes General Braddock was killed and almost all his force cut to pieces; one of the few who escaped was a handy solid fellow called George Washington who knew what to do when there were Indians about.

In order to be somewhere near on a level with the Indian guerrillas, the British Army had to form its first effective light infantry unit, who were called the Royal American Rifles. These men were given green coats to wear, instead of scarlet, black buttons instead of shining brass. It may seem strange to some modern soldiers, but they were forbidden to pipeclay their gear. (Blanco had not then been invented.) Naturally when George Washington threw us out of America the War Office disbanded the Royal American Rifles; but not long afterwards they found the need for similar troops as skirmishers, and the Rifle Brigade is the direct inheritor of the first modern soldiers clothed for invisibility and taught to fight as skirmishers and snipers.

The Americans, who had learnt from Indian savages and from shooting anything between squirrels and bears, fought largely as guerrillas during the first period of their War of Independence. The first action, at and near Lexington, was described by a British major as follows: "The Country by this time took ye Alarm and went immediately in Arms, and had taken their different stations behind Walls, etc., on our Flanks, and thus were we harassed in our Front, Flanks and Rear . . . it not being possible for us to meet a Man otherwise than behind a Bush, Stone hedge or Tree, who immediately gave his fire and off he went." (Field, *Echoes of Old Wars.*)

Throughout the whole of this war British and German

25

troops complained of the American guerrillas and skirmishers. These forces were unable to win battles; it was not until Washington had hammered into shape something like a real army, and had received the help of Regular troops from France, that the Americans were able to win decisive battles and campaigns. That is one of the clear things about guerrilla forces in modern war: they may be able to hold out, but they cannot win except in combination with striking forces that can meet the enemy in open battle.

When Napoleon was ruling about as much of Europe as Hitler is ruling now, the Spaniards began guerrilla fighting against his generals. There is no better description of guerrilla fighting available to the English reader than the two novels by C. S. Forester, *The Gun* and *Death to the French*. In these two novels we see the French Army strung out across the whole of Spain and so harassed by guerrillas that even the great main roads by which it lived could not be held safely against them. And we read also of the guerrilla adventures of a British Rifleman, one of the green-coated skirmishers trained by Sir John Moore, mainly on the basis of American experience, to form the incomparable Light Division and the skirmishing lines of Wellington's striking force. Here in the Peninsular War is an inspiring example of the combination between striking force and guerrilla. One would have been useless without the other. The guerrillas, after years of fighting, were never in a position to do more than raid. Wellington, after daring and skilful attacks on isolated sections of the French Army, was still after years of war so weak in force as compared with his opponents that he too had to adopt scorched earth tactics, and destroy most of a province of Portugal before he retired to the Lines of Torres Vedras. Behind these Lines he waited until the French Army opposite him was starved out; then he could come back again to meet and defeat French forces thinned out by their long effort to hold down the guerrillas.

It is worth remembering that example, because Wellington's men and the Spanish guerrillas played their part in a greater campaign. Napoleon went to Moscow. The Russians couldn't stop him. But they could burn their cities and they burnt even the holy city of Moscow. The flower and the spirit of Napoleon's army died in the terrible retreat from the Russian capital. He raised new troops and led them in enormous battles. But when in exile and defeat he grumbled that his army had never been the same again; and he remembered not only the mid-winter of Moscow but also "the Spanish ulcer"; the running sore that drained the strength of France.

In the next chapter, continuing the history of guerrilla warfare, we deal with fighting of this century. But it is worth while giving a paragraph or two to another form of fighting that is not very different from guerrilla war. The Navy should never be left out. British and American sailors, as pirates or privateers, or crews and masters of little ships, have often fought in seas and along shores dominated by an enemy. Drake singeing the King of Spain's beard, or John Paul Jones twisting the Lion's tail in British waters, are names to be remembered. What is the modern submarine but a weapon of naval guerrilla war and the corvette or armed merchantman that fights back? And just as in land warfare the civilian has his part to play, so the men of the merchant ships and of all sorts of curious vessels can do things that lie outside the text-books of war. Past the great warships and blockading forces of many nations they can run in with the supplies an army needs in its struggle against Fascism. I remember the very gallant men who served with Potato Jones, and other captains like him, bringing cargoes to Republican Spain. And they can scramble across the narrow seas in almost anything that floats, to rescue a British Army that a British government has left without the proper weapons with which to fight; they did that at Dunkirk.

When the British people are given the chance once more—as I hope they will be before this book is printed—

to do at least as much real fighting in this war as the Roumanians or Serbs are doing, I am sure that some of our guerrillas will be web-footed. And this is already the case with the special forces raised in Britain called Commandos. They are half soldiers, half marines, and wholly guerrilla. Their name derives from the Boer War. When the Boer armies had been defeated they split up into small "commandos" that carried on the struggle against large British armies for about a couple of years. The Boers taught us something, and it is good that we have not forgotten it.

CHAPTER III

THE greatest master of guerrilla warfare whose exploits and ideas are fully known to us was Lawrence of Arabia. There may be, in China or the Balkans, greater masters whom we do not at present know; meanwhile Lawrence can give us much of what we want. He describes his views of the Arab revolt he led, in his great book the *Seven Pillars of Wisdom*. Recovering from fever in an Arab tent he thought over what the Arabs wished to do—conquer perhaps 140,000 square miles held by the Turks. And he thought:

"How would the Turks defend all that? . . . no doubt by a trench line across the bottom, if we were an army attacking with banners displayed . . . but suppose we were an influence (as we might be), an idea, a thing invulnerable, intangible, without front or back, drifting about like gas? Armies were like plants, immobile as a whole, firm rooted, nourished through long stems to the head. We might be a vapour, blowing where we listed. Our kingdoms lay in each man's mind, and as we wanted nothing material to live on, so perhaps we offered nothing material to the killing. It seemed a regular soldier might be helpless with-

28

out a target. He would own the ground he sat on, and what he could poke his rifle at.

"Then I estimated how many posts they would need to contain this attack in depth, sedition putting up her head in every unoccupied one of these hundred thousand miles. I knew the Turkish Army inside and out, and allowing for its recent extension of faculty by guns and aeroplanes and armoured trains, still it seemed it would have need of a fortified post every four square miles, and a post could not be less than twenty men. The Turks would need six hundred thousand men to meet the combined illwills of all the local Arab people. They had one hundred thousand men available. It seemed the assets in this part of command were ours, and climate, railways, deserts, technical weapons could also be attached to our interests, if we realized our raw materials and were apt with them. The Turk was stupid and would believe that rebellion was absolute, like war, and deal with it on the analogy of absolute warfare. Analogy is fudge, anyhow, and to make war on rebellion is messy and slow, like eating soup with a knife."

Lawrence pointed out that "most wars are wars of contact, both forces striving to keep in touch to avoid tactical surprise. Our war should be a war of detachment . . . not disclosing ourselves until the moment of attack." This is the essence of guerrilla tactics, and at the time when Lawrence fought it was natural that these tactics should reach their highest level in the desert, where Regular forces cannot exist in large numbers to hold a continuous front. Today the aeroplane has altered the desert. It is no longer "the silent threat of a vast unknown desert." It is usually a patch of country where there is no cover from air observation. Abd el Krim fought well, only a few years after Lawrence. The air gave him away. Today the guerrilla must work more from the forest and from broken country than from the treeless spaces; more from centres of population than from the empty spaces. But the principles that Lawrence laid down hold good for this form of war today.

He pointed out that the ideal was never to give the enemy soldier a target. "Many Turks on our front had no chance all the war to fire a shot at us, and correspondingly we were never on the defensive except by a rare accident." And he laid down that this was only possible if intelligence about the enemy was perfect, "so that we could plan in complete certainty."

And Lawrence saw that political warfare, propaganda, is an essential part of this sort of war. "The printing press is the greatest weapon in the armoury of the modern commander," he wrote. "We had won a province when we had taught the civilians in it to die for our ideal of freedom: the presence or absence of the enemy was a secondary matter."

I cannot help applying those words to Europe to-day. And they are not the words of a foreigner or of someone in (someone who could ever have been in) a Ministry of Information. They are the words of the most remarkable English soldier known to the whole world. "We have won Europe when we have taught the civilians in it to die for our ideal of freedom: the presence or absence of Hitler's troops is a secondary matter."

Guerrilla attack, Lawrence noted, should be directed against whatever the enemy lacks most. The Turks were very short of material, and therefore his attacks were directed mainly against material. To attack the unguarded railway, the stores almost undefended, was also the best policy for him because his Arab troops would scarcely stand casualties. In war against the Nazis, whose method of warfare depends so much upon road transport and inflammable fuel and lubricating oil, it is clear that the guerrilla has many material targets of this sort. But towards the end of the Arab revolt, when the Turkish Army was breaking, Lawrence saw that the Arabs must be launched as a stinging swarm of raiders against the flank and rear of that army. While he was draining the Turkish strength, he liked to leave the Turkish railways just working, and not more than just working. When Allenby's striking force was ready for the decisive blow, Lawrence sent his Arabs to cut and hold the Turk's railway centres.

The guerrillas' target is chosen by the needs of battle, not by any absolute rule.

Captain Liddell Hart's book, *Colonel Lawrence,* is the best description of Lawrence as a soldier and guerrilla leader. In this book Captain Liddell Hart describes the final phase of the war in Palestine as one in which nearly half the Turkish forces south of Damascus were distracted by the Arabs. Two Turkish army corps, worn and wearied down until their strength, with that of the railway garrisons, was only about 14,000 fighting men, were pinned east of the Jordan. Liddell Hart writes: "The most remarkable feature is that, with some relatively light assistance from Chaytor's force, these Turkish masses were paralyzed by an Arab contingent that counted less than 3,000 men, and of which the actual expeditionary corps was barely 600 strong." Allenby's striking force only had to deal with the other half of the harassed and hopeless Turkish Army.

And summarizing the whole campaign, Liddell Hart writes: "The wear and tear, the bodily and mental strain, that exhausted the Turkish troops and brought them to breaking point was applied by the Arabs, elusive and ubiquitous, to a greater extent than by the British forces . . . They severed the line of communication at the moment when it became the life-and-death line, when the fate of the enemy hung on this frayed thread."

Summarizing the man Lawrence, Liddell Hart also writes: "Military history cannot dismiss him as merely a successful leader of irregulars. He is seen to be more than a guerrilla genius—rather does he appear a strategist of genius who had the vision to anticipate the guerrilla trend of civilized warfare that arises from the growing dependence of nations on industrial resources."

It will be a tragedy if the British people, having produced such a genius, fails to learn from him. And nothing was more astonishing in 1940 than to find that it was only our unofficial gang at Osterley Park who were talking about Lawrence's methods of warfare; in the newspapers

and in the training manuals and in lectures of high of
ficers, who tried to teach us to fight like gentlemen, nei
ther the Army, nor the Home Guard, nor the civilian was
given Lawrence as an example to think about and copy
What a queer country it is that produces such men, and
makes out of them heroes for boys but not teachers for
the "serious." The "serious" thing to do in modern war
if we are to judge from the efforts of officialdom, is to sit
in a block-house that is the most obvious feature of any
landscape and get what is coming to you. It is to be de
fensive all the time, and to count any attack on your
enemy as necessarily postponed until you have forces
equal in numbers and material strength to that enemy.
There would have been no Arab revolt if that had been
Lawrence's way of thinking.

Nor—to move on a few years—would the Irish Free State
ever have come into existence if the Irish had believed
that it was necessary, before they tackled Britain, to have
armaments equal to those of Britain. The Irish "Troubles" consisted of a guerrilla war fought by quite a small
section of the population, backed up by the majority of
the population. E. O'Malley's book, called in this country
On Another Man's Wound, and in America Army Without Banners, is almost as vivid and thrilling a description
of the risks and chances of guerrilla war as Denis Rietz'
Commando, the story of the Boers' guerrilla fighting. In
the Boers' case they had the advantage of mobility; they
were mounted infantry who could always ride round the
English infantry and could usually ride away from English cavalry. The Irish had no such advantage; they had
not even the relative mobility of Lawrence's men on
camels. But they realized that the streets of towns and
villages are good cover for the guerrilla and the sniper.
They did more roof-top fighting than any force before or
after them. And one of the best of O'Malley's stories includes a ladder propped up silently against the blank,
solid wall of a police station, and men silently removing

32

the slates from the roof of the building in order to pour in petrol and then throw in a match.

The Irish were the first guerrillas to fight against an army that largely manœuvred by vehicle. The British forces in Ireland used petrol-driven vehicles for movement and for supply. Against these vehicles the Irish developed their weapons and techniques. After a period, no unarmoured vehicle could be safely used in Ireland unless it was netted against the hand-grenade and was capable of using machine-gun fire at once—against guerrillas manning an ambush. How important a wastage this can be, from the point of view of a modern commander needing his trained men and his machine-guns for actual battle, can be seen when we realize that a modern motorized or mechanized unit may have one vehicle for every ten men, including machines needed for supply; and even infantry divisions not considered motorized will have about one vehicle for every 25 men. If all these vehicles must have machine-guns and skilled machine-gunners on board, for fear of guerrillas, the drain on the enemy's resources is enormous.

Naturally one of the main ways in which guerrillas use improvised or partly improvised weapons and tactics, against an army that moves by vehicle, is the use of high explosive in the form of mine or hand-grenade, and fire in the form of "Molotov cocktail" or flame-thrower. Some of these methods were developed in the war in Spain, not only for the attack on lorries but for the more difficult job of attacking tanks. The "dynamiteros" who first tackled Fascist tanks in Spain were mainly Asturians, to begin with, and they had learnt the tricks of guerrilla warfare in the Asturian revolt of 1934. This business of tank-hunting and tank-stopping is one of the ways in which guerrilla tactics have forced themselves into the accepted tactics of large-scale war. And the Spaniards showed that improvisation and the power to adopt new tactics is an essential factor if the Fascist war machine is to be held up.

There was not as much actual guerrilla war behind the enemy's lines in Spain as there might have been. The trouble was that the Republican Army had to be almost entirely improvised and could only be hastily trained. Therefore most of the best efforts of those who knew how to fight went into the training of this army, and into the battles which it fought; a casual, slipshod, amateur way of fighting had to be ended in order that the Republican armies might remain in being as a striking force. There were therefore too few people to plan and carry out guerrilla activity behind the enemy's lines. General Franco's forces had of course their own guerrillas, in the peculiar form typical of Nazi strategy. They had the Fifth Column. We had at one time what we called a "Phantom Brigade" which operated behind General Franco's lines in the south, where the fronts were relatively open. Hemingway's book *For Whom the Bell Tolls* describes guerrilla fighting north of Madrid. It was an essential element in our resistance to Fascism; if we had been able to develop it as successfully as we developed an army, that war might still be going on. And in that case this war we are now engaged in could never have started.

In one sense the struggle of the guerrillas in Spain has not ended yet, and does not look like ending. When General Franco's forces, at the beginning of his revolt, seized the area around Seville, some miners from the Rio Tinto mines and some peasants made their way into the hills. Right throughout the years of the war in Spain these isolated guerrillas maintained their hiding places and their raids. They are there still; they still raid.

Right in the north of Spain in the mountains of the Asturias, even stronger guerrilla forces held out for the Republic long after German bombers and Italian tanks had "conquered" the Republic of the Basques and its Asturian neighbours. Their ranks have been swelled by prisoners who have escaped from General Franco's overcrowded prison camps. As month after month and year after year General Franco has shown the population of

34

Spain that he has only leaden food to give them, these guerrillas in the hills have become of more importance. They cannot defeat the Nazi grip on Spain; they cannot even defeat Franco, a much weaker thing. But what they could do, combined with a striking force, seems to me likely to be on a level with what their ancestors did when combined with Wellington's men.

At the other end of the world a Republic exists as an independent state because its rulers did not think it necessary to stop fighting until it had enough tanks, and because its people fought as guerrillas even when the fighting front had gone far past them. The Chinese guerrillas have not only shown us new tactics; they have also solved some of the problems of supply for a guerrilla force. They have solved these problems in two ways. They have reduced to a fine art the business of getting arms and ammunition from their enemies. And secondly they have developed "guerrilla industry," little factories and workshops hidden and kept secret. They have made some of their essential industries portable, mobile, and so dispersed that they are not a good target for Japanese bombs or ground forces. It is one of the most extraordinary stories in the history of warfare, and it is told with skill and detail in Edgar Snow's *Scorched Earth*.

The Chinese guerrillas have even established a university behind the Japanese lines. They hold and operate from scores of counties, in which taxes are collected for the Chinese government and justice is administered by Chinese magistrates. In whole provinces of China—and some Chinese provinces are as big as France—the Japanese can only hold the railways and large cities. Outside these, Chinese life goes on under the protection of the guerrillas—and Japanese deaths go on.

China has a striking force as well as guerrillas, yet the long war there is a stalemate. This is because the Chinese armies have practically none of the weapons of a modern army. Because the guerrillas are so powerful and effective, even a small addition to the armament of the striking force might put the Chinese in a position to win back much of their enormous country, or even to drive the Japanese into the sea. At some point in this war's strategy that may be well worth considering.

When the story comes to be told of the reconquest of Abyssinia from the Italians, it seems certain that the same combination will be seen, between striking force and guerrillas, as in larger campaigns. Some of these guerrillas were organized and led by British officers, and two of these officers are known to us through American reports. One of them, Brigadier Sanford, had lived in Ethiopia for 30 years as a trader; he contributed, clearly, the local knowledge that is so invaluable to a guerrilla leader. Another of these officers, Major Orde Wingate, had trained and commanded Jewish irregulars in Palestine, until they could meet Arab raiders on equal terms. His contribution has clearly been the tricks and tactics of irregular war. Why the story of these and other men, a story that may be almost as great as that of Lawrence of Arabia, has been kept hidden from the British public is one of the mysteries of this war. It is an old maxim in war to learn from your enemies; but how curiously comatose are a people and an army that avoids learning even from its friends.

It is impossible to write of the history of guerrilla warfare without mentioning the history in the making today. The campaign in Russia is the greatest example of the use of mechanized force there ever has been in the world; it is also the greatest example of guerrilla war. Guerrilla fighting is no new thing to the Russians. After the last Great War, when the Red Army had scarcely any arms or equipment, the Soviet Union fought against the armies of 14 states invading Russia, and against Russian counter-revolutionaries. Much of the Red Army's fighting had to be done, necessarily, by guerrilla or, as the Russians call them, Partisan methods. They had not forgotten these Partisan methods when the Nazi armies invaded their country.

Because the newspapers have been full of Russian guerrilla fighting some people think that the Russians have discovered a new way of doing the job. But no accounts of really new methods have reached us. The last issue of *Soviet War News* to come my way reports that two Soviet Boy Scouts, aged 12 and 14, have been killing Nazi motorcyclists with a wire across a road. The British Boy Scouts who demonstrated how this should be done at Osterley, when we had not enough older instructors, were about the same age.

Perhaps there are no new methods of guerrilla warfare. Or perhaps new methods only grow up gradually as weapons and explosives change. As far as I can see, the things the Russians are doing, and doing very effectively, do not differ in essentials from the things we were teaching at Osterley in the summer of 1940.

The Osterley gang advocated the improvising of grenades out of cocoa tins; the defenders of Odessa used caviare tins. As the reports come through, we find our bag of tricks "discovered" one by one in the newspapers. We naturally should never have thought of caviare; but we had thought of the fact that even a highly mechanized modern army, fully equipped with all the latest stuff, would still need backing by improvisations made from the nearest handy material.

One thing stands out from the Russian reports that is only paralleled by the Chinese, and the Balkan guerrillas. After the Nazi army has stormed through an area and left it, in the burned villages and little towns the Soviet spring up again. One case has been reported of a Soviet pilot shot down in territory "occupied by the Nazis." He fell among friends, and found that the local soviets had been re-established under guerrilla protection as soon as the Nazi troops were drawn away for the offensive against Moscow. The pilot was injured and had to lie up for a period until he was fit enough to travel on the "underground railway" to rejoin his unit. When he was ready to leave, the officials of the local Soviet decided that he must have a proper medical certificate stating why he had been absent for so long, and on this certificate the proper rubber stamps and signatures were affixed.

That brings our rough outline of the past of guerrilla warfare right up to today. But we can see also the shape of things to come in other news that reaches us as this book is being written. *The Times* states that there are a hundred thousand insurgents in one little Balkan country, Yugoslavia. As this book is completed further news comes of a regular soldier, Colonel Mihailovich, who leads an "invisible army" blockading Belgrade, holding at least a quarter of Serbia and in possession of three aerodromes. It is no longer a question of a future potential outbreak of guerrillas in Europe; they have established already in the Balkans the "Second Front" that Britain still discusses. There are men fighting still in Poland; from angry Norway and unhappy France comes news of the rising movement of revolt. And these guerrillas are not all "mountainy men"; great cities like Prague and Oslo show signs of the planning and organization that may at the right time burst out into strikes, street fighting, the seizure of arsenals and Nazi stores of arms, the growth of city guerrillas. That clearly can be the shape of the future—if and when there is a striking force to do its share of the job.

CHAPTER IV

WHEN we read about guerrilla warfare in the days gone by—about, for example, guerrilla bands in Spain operating against Napoleon's forces—there is one thing which stands out. These bodies were hastily improvised; they sprang up spontaneously *after* the invader had been operating for some time. Yet they were very effective.

How much more so, then, had they been prepared—had

38

they learned beforehand the technique of guerrilla fighting, and studied the terrain in which they were going to operate.

We have a valuable advantage over these guerrillas o. history. We are not yet invaded—we may never be—but we can be prepared. We can begin right now to survey our local territory, to learn the tactics of guerrilla warfare, to practise the ruses and stratagems by which the enemy may be weakened and obstructed.

I would impress upon every potential defender of this country, every member of the population who is fitted to take part in guerrilla fighting, every Home Guard unit, the golden precept: *be prepared!* Instead of having hastily to form our fighting bands, on the spur of the moment, and then to lose time locating favourable spots for headquarters, hiding-places, rallying and dispersal points; instead of having to learn the methods of organized guerrilla fighting by painful and arduous rule-of-thumb trial and error, let us start right now.

What is the first requirement in this preparedness? Guerrilla fighters operate in their own particular section of the countryside, on their own hills and highways, in and around their own towns and villages. Therefore the first requirement is: know your own territory, and know it both by day and by night.

The importance of knowing every foot of one's own territory cannot be over-estimated. Whether it be the rugged, wooded hills of North Britain, or the pastures, hop-fields and gentle contours of Kent, whether it be the narrow coal-mining valleys of South Wales or the fens and broads of East Anglia or any populous manufacturing district where only thin strips of countryside separate one smoky town from another—if it is your district you must learn to know it like a book. Or better than a book, for how many of us can remember on just what page or line a certain expression occurs, in even the most frequently read volume?

Get your local bearings. Learn to be able to say, at a

second's notice, wherever you may be walking or riding, which is the south, north, east and west. Know in what direction every road runs, not merely its compass direction but to what town it runs and through what valleys, plains and hamlets, and over what hills. Make yourself acquainted with field-paths and short cuts, and with the kind of cover they possess—hedges, trees, ditches, etc.

Find out the points in your territory which make the best observation posts, from which wide views may be obtained. Classify them according to the time of day when they will be most useful. A good post in the morning, with the sun rising in the east behind you and illuminating the terrain in front, may be useless in the evening when the lateral rays of the sun strike you full in the eyes, half-blinding you, and perhaps making concealment doubly difficult.

"Classify them," I have just said. This means taking notes. Not any and every individual carrying a bunch of notes around with him, but your Section Leader (if you are a Home Guard) or other commander should receive all such useful material and arrange it in orderly form. But every individual should memorize as much as possible, for you never know when you may be separated from your leader, or lose him in action. Deliberately set about training your memory. There is no more valuable gift than a memory for detail. Walk into a room. Remain there two or three minutes, noting its contents. Then go into another room. Sit down and write out every object you can remember seeing. Keep this up, and you will find that your power to retain detail is increasing. To depend too much upon written notes is dangerous, for your notes might fall into unauthorized hands. There are some things—such as caches, hide-outs and so on, to which we shall refer later—whose location must never be written down.

When you take a walk or a cycle ride in a part of your territory which is not well known to you, keep your eyes skinned for detail, for the lay of the land. Look back frequently as you go forward, so as to impress upon your mind the roads and landmarks for the return journey. Don't forget that, if you don't look back, you will remember only what *one side* of a house or a hill or a copse looks like, and that is the side which won't be of any use to you on the way back.

Not only should you learn the outlines of buildings and other marks, from all sides. You should know what they look like from a lower sight-level—when you are lying down. For the day may come when you cannot stand up to look for these landmarks; you will be crawling low through cover. You will be surprised to find the difference there sometimes is in the view of a thing from a standing and a prone position.

You can practise this by day and night, on your way to work or on your evening or Sunday walks. Keep your eyes skinned and your memory keen. You cannot know every foot of your territory, but you can make that your ideal and aim for it. Mark every road, path, copse, shrubbery, bit of bracken, hill, hedge, valley, railway line, tunnel, culvert, power station, church steeple, isolated cottage or house, river or stream, pond, lake; and note, by compass, how they lie. And every indentation, dip and hollow, and the winding course of streams.

This observation of your territory is not only in order to enable you to move about swiftly and accurately. Many of these objects will serve you later for cover, observation posts, hiding places, bases for attack, etc. Some of them will be the objects of enemy attack, which you may try to prevent or drive off. Power stations, telephone exchanges, post offices, factories where war materials are produced—all these are objectives for enemy attack, places which he may want either to destroy or to use in order to communicate, or cut your communications, or to spread false news.

Every area and object in your territory which you have learned to know by day, you must learn to know by night. It is not enough to study the areas and landmarks in your

41

territory by day, and hope that you will recognize them by night. Things look too different in the darkness.

Learn to know things by bright moonlight and on moonless nights. Technically speaking—according to the calendar—there are only 12 nights of complete darkness in the year. But there are many other nights—by no means rare in our British climate!—in which the moon is obscured by clouds, mist, fog or rain, giving you maybe a hundred black nights in the year. On such nights, direction is hard to find. This makes it imperative that you should make yourself acquainted with things which aid direction, by sight or by feel. Note the different forms of fencing of every farm and field—hedges, stone walls, barbed wire, palings, etc.—and the direction in which these boundaries lie. Then when you come into contact with them you will know where you are, if you get turned and twisted around when attacked.

Your sense of touch must also be used in finding your way at night, as well as your sense of hearing and of smell. Pig-styes, cowsheds, breweries, tanneries, all have their distinguishing fragrance—if I may use the term—and their scent will help you to locate yourself. The ripple of a brook or the croaking of frogs in a certain pond or pool— all these things, carefully memorized on your nightly excursions, may in the future help you to find your way at night when finding your way is a matter of life or death, life for you and death for the enemy.

Another point to bear in mind is to memorize every bit of "dead ground" in your district. This is territory which, by its natural conformation, is shielded from the enemy's view and fire. Such territory is very suitable for guerrillas to pass through, or in which to rest. It is also eminently suitable for luring the enemy into prepared traps, where we can deal with them without being observed by their larger units. While there are not many pieces of *perfect* dead territory—which the enemy cannot observe from any angle or direction, except perhaps from an aeroplane— there are many which may be "dead" from the east, or the north, south or west. You must remember from which direction these areas are "dead," so that later you can use them—once you know the location of the enemy.

Every Home Guard unit should have a sand table of its defense area. This, as you probably know, is a sort of relief map or scale model in sand of your district: you can construct it yourselves and you can continually modify and improve it as your knowledge of the area grows. You construct on it the hills and valleys, indicating streams by using paper or tin-foil, trees by planting matchsticks with green paper foliage, cardboard houses, and so on. This should be kept in the Home Guard centre or hut, and studied exhaustively.

It is not only the country roads, the woods, hills and valleys, which you must study. You must know also the towns and villages in your district. The enemy will not keep to the countryside. He will endeavour to occupy the populated centres. Here also you can carry on guerrilla warfare, sniping, ambushing, blowing him up. You must know the general street plan of the towns or villages. You must know every entrance and exit to them also—not only the main roads, with their tank obstacles, but every side street or pathway leading into the town. Not merely to keep the enemy out, but also so that you can sneak in and out when he is there, or near.

You must know which houses in the towns or villages can best be adapted for conversion into observation posts, strong points or hiding places. We do not want to postpone till the day of need the selection of the buildings which will be used in this manner.

Find out about the drainage system of important factories, whether by means of it you can enter the factory when the enemy is in occupation, to commit acts of sabotage. Don't forget to examine the coal-chutes of the local power station—a hefty charge of explosive can be sent down into the building by this route. A lump of clay with explosive embedded in it and coal dust patted thoroughly into the outside looks exactly like a lump of coal. Such a charge can be dropped down a coal-chute or on to a pile of coal. Firemen will then shovel it into the fire-box with the ordinary coal and up goes your power house.

Know how to enter important or strong buildings without using the main entrances, also what buildings have convenient secondary exits—chutes, windows, or what-have-you—to use if you want to make a rapid detour or get-away. Note which is the blind side of the building. Get the lay-out of the city sewers—you may not like the idea, but one day you may find them handy for under-

ground roadways. The borough or county engineer or his employees ought to tell the Home Guard all they want to know about this. He can warn you how to avoid being poisoned by sewer gas, against which gas masks are useless.

And this brings me to another point. Not only must we get to know our territory. We must get to know people. People who can be of use to us, who have an intimate knowledge of some aspect or other of our territory. Men and women who can give us useful information now, and who will give us invaluable information if ever the enemy is all around. But if we are to expect their help then, we

44

must get to know them now, so that we can contact them easily, and they will trust us in a time when a man's life may be forfeit for aiding guerrillas. And all A.R.P. men, firemen and others—who may become guerrillas—should be instructed by the Home Guard in the use of arms.

It should be part of our preparedness campaign to get to know employees of the public services, rural and city postmen, policemen, A.R.P. personnel, milk roundsmen, errand boys, lorry-drivers, firemen, gamekeepers, district nurses, innkeepers and others—people who know our territory, and people who are in touch with the inhabitants, who hear rumours of what is afoot, and can relay information regarding the enemy. An A.R.P. warden probably knows something of every household in his section. Errand boys can carry verbal messages when on their rounds, and so on.

Home Guard officers should also get to know the regular army units in their areas. They should, if possible, know the officers and non-commissioned officers personally. Invite them to your homes. Find some common ground for acquaintanceship. Let Home Guard men and regular army privates fraternize as much as possible. Organize sporting and social events. Let the Home Guards familiarize themselves with the faces of the officers, and with the regimental marks on the men's and officers' shoulders.

Then, if the enemy lands, and a unit in captured British uniforms comes marching down the street, with the familiar regimentals on their uniforms, look at the officers' and non-coms' faces—if they are all strange, you are entitled to smell a rat, or—which is the same thing—smell a Nazi. But, if you have made no attempt to become acquainted with officers and men in these local units, you might never know—until it was too late.

Both in town and country, it is worth while noting spots which you can use as hide-outs or temporary headquarters or bivouacs when guerrilla war begins. While you can never be sure that the enemy won't get there first,

45

you should select places to which he is unlikely to penetrate during his advance, or for some time after his occupation.

Then there is the important matter of caches, or hiding-places for arms, ammunition and supplies. We are living in the days of *Blitzkrieg*—"lightning war"—remember, and the enemy is not going to allow us time to select suitable spots and to bury our stores, after he has landed from the sea or dropped from the air.

I suggest that Home Guard units bury boxes, four feet long and six to eight inches wide and deep, under disused culverts, in wells, cisterns, hollow trees, caves, etc. These boxes should be well lined as protection against damp. In them you can hide clothing—civilian clothes for disguise, for instance—and the "invisible weapons" which I describe in a later chapter. If the Home Guards are ever surrounded by the enemy they can exchange their uniforms for these civilian clothes, and hide their "visible weapons." Emergency rations and first-aid kits can also be kept in these caches.

Preparedness does not consist only of knowledge, for knowledge is useless without practice. I therefore strongly recommend that Home Guards be given plenty of exercises which will test their knowledge of their territory and also prepare them for guerrilla warfare. Those units of the Home Guard which lay all emphasis on drills, route marches and other exercises which are identical with those of the regular army are making a sad mistake, that they may regret when it is too late.

There are many games and exercises specially designed to develop alertness, sense of direction, and other qualities essential to the guerrilla fighter. Some of these are Boy Scout games; we should never be ashamed to learn from the Boy Scouts.

For example, let a group of men go to some point in a strange district at night and have them find their way back in the dark. Repeat this exercise a week later, to discover how much each man remembers of the route. Or have your men sit with their backs to a road, along which soldiers are marching, and estimate the number of men who have passed by, from sound alone. In later chapters, on guerrilla fighting, stalking and scouting, I describe a few games suitable for training. There are many more. You should start to play these games right now.

And one last preparedness point, for Home Guards only. In the old days when the rifle was first introduced to the Indian in America, he would never take two steps without it. He used to say, "My rifle is my mother, it feeds

me, it houses me, clothes me and protects me." Where-upon the white men called the Indians sons of guns, and thus this common expression was coined. All Home Guardsmen should be sons of guns—their rifles should always be ready to hand.

When the Nazis come over in their belly-crashing planes and gliders, or drop with parachutes, they may land in a hundred places at once. And you may be the one unit of fire-power to hold them up while the Home Guard rallies and the regulars are approaching.

So, whether you go to a tea-party or to work on your allotment, or to your office, factory, shop or field, take your rifle with you. When you go upstairs to bed, take it with you. Don't leave it downstairs for a German to grab if he enters the house. You may have to leave your house by the roof or window. Keep your rifle oiled and clean, and have some ammunition always by you. If you love your home and family, you must love your rifle, for it will help to protect them. If ever you *must* leave your rifle some place, hide it well, first taking out the bolt which you will either carry with you or hide in another place. Your ammunition should be hidden in yet another spot. You can't be too careful, but you certainly can be too careless.

CHAPTER V

WHEN the time comes, and the enemy attacks these shores by sea and his troops land from planes and gliders, you will know—if you have been prepared—how to act. Guerrilla warfare, is warfare within territory occupied by the enemy. But guerrilla methods can also be used to help stem his advance. In fact, movement of modern forces is so swift that it is hard to make a rigid distinction between these two stages: advance and occupation.

Of course, you may say, "It may never happen." But that is a dangerous state of mind if it leads us to neglect preparedness. You remember how, in the early days of the war, instructions were flashed on the cinema screens on how to act in an air raid, and at the end it said, "It may never happen." But it did—and how! Had we neglected air raid precautions, how much less would we have been prepared to face up to the bombing.

Besides this, the lessons of guerrilla fighting will be invaluable when our counter-offensive begins on the Continent.

48

The enemy, then, is on our soil. The course of the fighting has been such that, in some parts, the Home Guards and others must have recourse to guerrilla warfare.

As guerrilla fighters we do not expect to engage in pitched battles with the enemy forces. That would be suicidal—and it most certainly would not be guerrilla warfare. That is the job of the regular army. The activities of the guerrilla bands will consist of: observing the enemy and his movements (reconnaissance and scouting), obstructing the enemy's movements, and harassing the enemy by surreptitious or surprise action.

Observation of the enemy is not only essential to guerrilla fighters, so that they may know when to attack and when not to; when to shift quarters; it is also very useful to gain knowledge of enemy positions, numbers, units, etc., to relay to our regular troops.

Obstruction we shall deal with later, when we study ambushing and the destruction of communications. Under harassing we can include both the killing of the enemy and the destruction of his war material.

If we have studied and practised and exercised, as advised in the previous chapter, we shall be able to assume the rôle of guerrilla fighters, when this becomes necessary, swiftly and with a minimum of effort and error.

Let us hope by this time we have grasped the essential qualities of guerrilla fighting, namely: Caution, invisibility and surprise. We cannot properly employ these qualities unless we have initiative and obedience.

It may seem strange to you that I put caution first; that I do not even mention courage. Courage is the commonest of qualities. In my experience I have met very few real cowards, and they were probably sick men—nervously or psychologically—who would have responded to the right kind of expert treatment. Most men are naturally brave, just as most men also get scared. I have done my share of fighting, and I have been good and scared quite a few times. As an

American colonel said in the last war, "Nine out of ten men get scared in action, some time or other, and the tenth is a damned liar!" Maybe the tenth isn't a liar, but perhaps there is something just as wrong with him as with the apparently incurable coward. The stimulation of danger almost always develops courage.

But caution—real caution, not fear or panic—unlike courage, is a quality that must be deliberately cultivated and studied. The really difficult thing is to get a man to use his head when hell is popping. That takes real control. In guerrilla warfare, the good fighter is not the crazy hot-head who dashes into the scrap without a single thought as to how he is going to extricate himself afterwards. That type makes me more scared than the enemy does, because he usually gets himself killed and, what is worse, his companions also.

The good guerrilla fighter must out-smart, out-think, the other fellow. He needs plenty of audacity, but audacity should only be used after he has studied every possibility of a get-away as carefully as he has studied the attack. We cannot afford to throw away guerrilla fighters. There are not too many of them. It is their job to badger the enemy, to wreak as much destruction as possible, and then to withdraw and prepare for the next attack. If you know, when you go into action, that every possible step has been taken for you to get away into safety when that action is over—whether you have won or lost it—you will fight much better, more coolly, and therefore more effectively. The ideal guerrilla fighter is the man who keeps cool, with his mind working all the time, under circumstances in which most people couldn't think at all. "Guerrillas attack to annihilate and rove to keep from being annihilated," say the Chinese guerrilla leaders.

The courageous and successful partisans in China, who have been fighting behind the Japanese lines for years, have some good rules of tactics with regard to this. I quote some of them, as told by a famous Chinese partisan leader to Edgar Snow, in an interview reported by him in his book, *Red Star Over China:*

"Partisans must not fight any losing battles. Unless there are strong indications of success, they should refuse any engagement.

"Surprise is the main offensive tactic of the well-led partisan group. Static warfare must be avoided. . . .

"A careful and detailed plan of attack, and especially of retreat, must be worked out before any engagement is offered or accepted. Any attack undertaken without full preliminary precautions opens the partisans to outmanœuvre by the enemy. Superior manœuvring ability is a great advantage of the partisans, and errors in its manipulation mean extinction."

So much for caution. The second essential quality, invisibility, is obviously linked up with the first. Maintaining invisibility is really part of caution.

Invisibility is the guerrilla's fortress. The only one he can hope for. Steel and concrete can be shattered by high explosives, but how can you blast invisibility? Of what use heavy artillery or dive-bombers against ghosts or will-o'-the-wisps? The guerrilla keeps moving, seldom staying in one place for more than a night unless he has, in wild or mountainous country, an unusually secure stronghold. He is everywhere and nowhere; he strikes, one day here, the next day there. He knows how to take cover and how to camouflage himself and his belongings.

Do not forget—as a guerrilla you must be a dim but sinister shadow, a mosquito in a darkened tent that stings first here then there, his victims unable to trap him. Silent, lurking in tiny bands in river-beds, ditches, ravines, hillsides, empty railway cars, flitting from cover to cover, and like a gadfly pricking the bulky body of the enemy force, striving to goad it into wastage of effort and material.

Our third essential quality is surprise. These are basic guerrilla tactics: surprise and subterfuge. Surprise, to take the enemy unawares; subterfuge, to trick him by various ruses into doing the wrong thing, miscalculating your strength or position. Surprise attacks get on the enemy's

51

nerves. Our aim as guerrillas is to prevent the enemy spreading out to get control of territory. We try to keep him bunched up closely together. Numerically and in equipment, the enemy is always stronger than are the guerrillas. It is the surprise factor that equalizes us during our brief hit-and-run conflicts, in which our aim is to inflict the maximum of damage with a minimum of loss to ourselves.

Finally, among the required qualities of the guerrilla are initiative, team-work and obedience. Automatons, fighting robots, are useless as guerrillas. Each man must be able to think for himself, for he may at any time become separated from his comrades. At any time he may have to take charge of his group, if their leader is lost. Quick, clear thinking is essential, and then the rapid execution of your plan.

Every guerrilla leader worth his salt encourages initiative among his men. Before executing a coup of some kind —an attack on an enemy patrol, an ambush of an enemy convoy, or whatever it may be, the leader will explain clearly to the group the job ahead of them; he will outline the tactics to be used, and will ask for criticism and alternative suggestions. Thus every man will have a part in planning the forthcoming action. Through such discussion the members of the band have a full understanding of what is required of them, and also confidence in their leader and their own ability to do the job. This method is genuinely democratic, and it also happens to be the most effective, as democratic methods often are.

Once the plan is agreed on—in case of differences, the leader must always have the deciding voice—the members of the group must obey implicitly the orders of their leader. Discussion is excellent *before* action, and will happen in any case after action, but once action is decided upon the group must work like a perfect mechanism, actuated by the leader. Initiative plus discipline—this is the right combination for the competent guerrilla fighter.

CHAPTER VI

Now the enemy has occupied our particular area and is seeking to extend the district under his control. We guerrillas have taken to the woods, the hills, or some other place of hiding. We have a certain amount of equipment and are ready to operate. Now is the time to make use of what we have learned in our exercises, and to translate into action our principles of caution, invisibility, and surprise.

I am often asked, when lecturing, what size a guerrilla force should be. It is impossible to give a hard-and-fast answer to this question as it depends upon so many circumstances: the sort of cover you have, the particular job you wish to do, etc. In an area of open spaces—moors and downland, extensive woodlands, with hills and valleys—guerrillas can work in sections and companies, even up to battalion strength. But when towns and villages are situated more closely together, more caution and smaller numbers will be needed. There are certain jobs—sabotage, blowing up bridges, etc., when covering fire is not much needed, or stalking and reconnoitring operations—when the party of three to five men is best. There may be jobs which can best be done by one man alone, or by two. In a party of three, the centre man will do the job, while the other two, one on each side of him, are his "covers," helping, if need be, by noises or tricks to distract the enemy's attention, so that he may get through to his job. They also protect the man who will do the job. The distance to be maintained between the centre man and his two flanking companions depends upon the terrain and cover, the type of action contemplated, the position and strength of the enemy, the number and whereabouts of the enemy's sentries, and so on.

In the case of an action which is bound to bring down the enemy, perhaps before the job is finished, the men doing the actual work will need a covering party to hold up the enemy, and to give them more time. An example of this well worth studying is the account of the blowing up of a bridge by a party of Spanish Republican guerrillas, in Ernest Hemingway's novel, *For Whom the Bell Tolls.*

Then there is the question of the guerrillas' headquarters—the place from which they will operate. Here is another matter upon which it is impossible to be explicit. It depends upon the number of guerrillas, the nature of the country, the extent of the enemy's control over it, etc.

Sometimes you can establish headquarters on a comparatively permanent basis, in mountainous and heavily wooded country. In these circumstances you can post sentries and can decamp before the enemy can catch you. A cave is an excellent hiding place for a guerrilla band, or a small clearing in a wood—if you stick to its edges because of aeroplanes—a farmhouse or shepherd's hut on a lonely hill. In more populated areas, guerrillas may live in the town or village—apparently peaceful citizens—but going out one by one silently by night to their appointed meeting place to do their work. Many Chinese are farmers in the day-time and guerrillas at night.

54

Not many guerrillas can hope for the luxury of a semi-permanent headquarters. Most of them must make do with bivouacs which seldom remain on the one spot for more than two or three nights. Many guerrillas will never stay more than one night in each place—whether in the woods, on the hills or in a barn or village house—either a deserted one or one whose occupants are trustworthy. In the days of the "Troubles" in Ireland, the Irish Republican fighters made a point of shifting their sleeping-place every night—this was called being "on the run." They managed to do quite a lot of damage while "running."

Now is the time for you to discover places suitable for guerrilla bases and hide-outs. Once you have found them, and memorized their location, don't go near them. You never know who may observe you, and later—willingly or unwillingly—give information to the enemy.

In selecting any kind of base, there is one essential thing to look for: it must have a good get-away—a good way out to safety if discovered or attacked; preferably more than one get-away.

If you have a permanent base, or even a headquarters which is good for several days, you will have to make caches. These should contain spare ammunition, extra supplies, and so on. Some should be made before the enemy's landing, as I have recommended in Chapter IV. They should contain changes of clothing, uniforms—so that you can have the right outfit for every job—and also "invisible weapons," the kind of weapons which a guerrilla in civilian clothes can carry without attracting attention. They must be easily portable and easily concealed. First among these is the pistol. Then there are ladies' hat-pins (the old-fashioned kind, not so easily obtainable nowadays, but borrow one from Grandma). Daggers, blackjacks, knuckle-dusters, hammers, a roll of copper coins sewn into a piece of canvas or strong linen, a sock with the foot full of sand; all are useful These are all weapons which will silently put a man out, with the exception of the pistol, though the butt-end of this is a mean weapon. These are permanent caches, for continual use. When you are moving around, you may also require caches for your packs (if you are carrying any) extra food, and such-like, while you are absent on some scouting or destructive job.

A cache must be made sufficiently large to accommodate what you have to hide; you may have to make more than one. Be sure you don't pick a place into which water drains. If you have time, you can cover the sides of the cache with twigs or small branches interwoven with other twigs or brush. If all ground-sheets are not in use, wrap them round the bundles in the cache to protect them further against damp. Be careful to obliterate all traces of digging. If you can plant a bush or shrub over them so that it looks natural, do so; but if it doesn't look natural it is far worse than leaving the place naked. Obliterate tracks leading to and from the caches, and those around a bivouac.

Some woodcraft experts advise the marking of the cache by planting a stake nearby, with the bark removed, to show up in the darkness. One of these stakes is then notched, each notch representing one pace of the distance from stake to cache. This would be a good idea, if it were not for the fact that stakes stripped of their bark also show up well to enemy eyes. The German may have read books on woodcraft too, and he doesn't have to know the English language to be able to count notches on a stake. No, I am afraid you will have to choose the more difficult way, and memorize the position of your cache by its relation to stones, bushes, trees or other objects near by.

You must have your headquarters properly guarded. Post sentries in pairs, if your numbers are strong enough. They should be concealed, and able to cover every means of access to the camp; they should be able to communicate with each other without having to move about. Have frequent reliefs so that sentries do not get over-tired, when their alertness suffers and their eyes become over-strained.

Sentries should challenge strangers in clear tones, but not loudly. And they should wait till the last possible moment before challenging. Wait till you are satisfied—or almost satisfied—that the strangers are enemies, and that they are approaching so closely that they are bound to discover the camp. If an enemy scout approaches he should be dispatched, if possible, silently with a rifle-butt, blackjack or other instrument. By firing you will warn the rest of his party. As soon as an enemy is put out of action, sentries should inform the leader of their party, who will doubtless arouse his men.

Don't forget the use of camouflage in masking bivouacs or headquarters. Guerrillas will not be able to employ structural camouflage or carry stocks of canvas and paint around with them. You must make do with branches of trees, foliage, uprooted and re-planted bushes, sand or rocks. When branches become withered, replace them. The mouth of a cave should be concealed with rocks or branches, and you can have a piece of well-dirtied sacking over the door into which twigs and leaves are stuck. Never forget that camouflage means using colours and objects which blend with the natural surroundings. Nor must you let shadow betray the presence, say, of a machine-gun. Cover it so that it is unobserved from above—always keep aeroplane reconnaissance in mind when camouflaging: the enemy may appear above you, or on any side. Arrange your camouflage so that it casts a shadow of broken outline on the ground, similar to a bush or clump of bushes. Always take care that tracks leading to and from your headquarters or bivouac are covered or obliterated. It is sometimes worth while making false tracks not far from where you are situated, leading away from your position, and, preferably, ending at a stream or on rocky ground.

CHAPTER VII

BUT headquarters or bivouacs—whether comfortable or otherwise—are not places for us to stay in. We guerrillas are not out for a rest cure but to fight. Our headquarters, then, are merely bases from which we work, and often, when on a scouting or other mission, we shall not return to our base, if any, for days at a time.

The two things we must bear in mind when travelling are invisibility and silence. We must not be seen nor must we be heard. The necessity for concealment and stillness must so saturate our minds that we never make a movement without automatically taking advantage of cover—whether of irregularities of the land, of objects, or of shadow—nor without guarding against any revealing noise.

Move always in the shadows, even going out of your way to follow them. Remember that the longer way round

under cover is better than the shorter route if you are exposed. Take advantage of every bush, of trees, of slopes in the ground which lie between you and the enemy. Avoid moving along the top of a ridge or slope, for then you will be silhouetted against the sky-line. Don't cross the crest of a hill but work round it, a little lower than the highest point. If you must cross a hill-crest or ridge, you should crawl.

If you think you have been observed by the enemy at long range, freeze suddenly into immobility, not trying to move away while he is watching you. He may not be quite sure, and your movements, in trying to disappear, may confirm his suspicions. When you think he is no longer suspicious, move very slowly away to the flank or the rear. If your companions are still under cover they will realize what is happening, the moment they see you standing stock-still, and they also will remain motionless.

Whether you are walking, crouching, crawling or "snaking," your movements should be deliberate and slow. Never move jerkily. The world of nature is usually in continuous motion, even on the calmest day, and particularly in this country where breezes hardly ever fail. Slow, flowing movement on your part will harmonize with the move-

ments of the growth around or behind you. If you are lying down or crawling on all-fours, keep your feet on the ground and do not stick your behind up in the air.

Do not forget that your uniform is designed to blend with the prevailing colours of the countryside. If you wear civilian clothes, choose things of a neutral colour, brown or dark grey—not white, light grey, black or navy blue. A rain-coat is almost invariably khaki coloured, and therefore makes for good concealment. If your coat, trousers and waistcoat are of different shades, all the better. When you use shadow for concealment, never forget your background. If you stand in a shadow cast from one side of you, but with sunlight behind you, the shadow does not help. Either you must have behind you the object which casts the shadow—a wall or tree or whatever it is—or, if the shadow is cast from one side, it should be continuous behind you for some way, as the shadow cast by a hedge, for instance.

When scouting or stalking, never look directly at the sun, especially when it is low. To avoid this, it is well worth devoting some extra time to approach your objective from a different direction.

You can assist the process of concealment by using personal camouflage. Your uniform, or even dull-coloured civilian clothing, are the beginnings of camouflage; but we can add to this. Immobility is also a form of camouflage, as you will know if you have ever noted how a brilliantly coloured bird—such as a cock pheasant—can remain unobserved merely by remaining perfectly still.

If you have no personal camouflage, you can at least remember that you should never raise your hands and face so that the light catches them, either by day or night.

If you are wearing a tin hat, it will, of course, be painted a matt brown colour. But you can further conceal it by having a piece of sacking, veiling or netting over it in which are bits of green and brown rag, or feathers or leaves. Sometimes you will find it advisable to carry your steel helmet in your hand when negotiating close brush.

Carry a piece of burnt cork with you. Your memories of childhood days, when you played amateur blackface minstrels—if ever you did; it might have been engine-drivers, policemen or aviators—will recall the reason why. With it you can smear strips of black across your face, neck, ears and hands—which are the first to show up if you are observed from a distance. If you have no burnt cork, use some water from your water-bottle or a stream mixed with dirt to make mud to smear on your face and hands. You can use pulped berries or wild flowers too. Perhaps now you will begin to realize that the Indians' war-paint was not always meant for decoration. If you don't shave for a while—and you may find it hard to do so when scouting!—this will also help to break up the outlines of that treacherous white blob, your face. A khaki handkerchief across the face, tied just below the eyes, is another camouflaged trick, but it is rather a nuisance as it may keep on slipping. Of course, you will never carry a white handkerchief.

If you wear stout brown gloves or gauntlets you will not need to colour your hands. They are also a protection if you have to handle a lot of stiff and prickly gorse, thorn hedges, etc.

But guerrillas have to travel fast and light, and therefore cannot carry much in the way of equipment. So for most of our camouflage we must borrow from nature. We can use leaves upon our shoulders as well as upon our hats. Don't forget that all leaves have two colours: the underside is always lighter than the upper side. Have the dark side uppermost in your personal camouflage.

Bracken, when brown, also makes good camouflage wear. You can pin a few twigs on to your clothes, here and there, if you like, or pieces of bark—this will blend with the shades and shadows at all hours of the day.

Carry nothing with you that can reflect light, if possible. If you wear eyeglasses, you can't do much about that, but avoid having them reflect the sun. The same applies to the lenses of binoculars, which can be covered with a thin spider-web veiling. Have all metal objects painted black or brown. Don't try to be too spick-and-span, as, the cleaner objects are, the more likely are they to reflect light or show up whitely. Alternate strips of black and white tape on your rifle will help to disguise it.

Play a camouflage game right now, if you like. Go into the woods and camouflage yourself, then appear at certain points, previously specified, and have your companions note down the exact minute when they observe you at these points—if they do observe you.

When standing beside a tree, keep your legs close together. If you stand with them apart, you can be seen easily. Don't forget also that branches or twigs, striking against your tin hat, can be heard some distance away, so you may have to carry it.

When walking, always lift your foot well clear of the ground as when "marking time," then put it down again flatly, neither toe first nor heel first. Never walk on tip-toe, and never slide your feet along the ground. Naturally you will avoid as far as possible treading on dry leaves or sticks, or disturbing stones. If you must cross twigs and dry leaves, or make your way through undergrowth, wait for a breath of wind to rustle the leaves around you. Never smash your way through undergrowth, but lift it upward or aside bit by bit and creep underneath it.

If you are proceeding behind a low fence or hedge, it may be sufficient to crouch, so as to be below its line. But there are occasions when you will have to crawl. Crawling is a slow, irksome business and I always avoid it if I can, preferring to take a somewhat longer way round where I can walk. If you must crawl, you should adopt one of two forms of crawling according to circumstances. The first is the cat-crawl on all fours. If the ground is covered with dry leaves or twigs it is best to rest your right knee where your right hand was and so on. This lessens the amount of noise you make. When carrying a rifle always set it down ahead of you each time you advance a pace. Make sure that the safety catch is on.

The side-crawl is very useful. Lie down on your left side with your left leg doubled and your right leg over your left, with your right knee resting on the ground just below the left one. Then use the inside of right foot as a sort of piston to shove yourself forward, keeping the left knee doubled all the time and your left forearm also helping to pull you forward. In this position the muzzle of your rifle rests on your right hand and you can carry your rifle or other weapon on the inside of the left thigh. You can throw a grenade from this position by raising your body slightly with the aid of the left hand as a prop, rolling backward from the hips and propelling yourself forward on your left knee.

Another kind of crawl is the belly-crawl. This form of progression is also called "snaking." It must be done with a gradual, flowing movement, not jerkily, and I cannot tell you how to do it; you can only learn by trying.

If you can, have the sun at your back in the early morning, and in the evening when it is low. Then the enemy must look into the sun when he looks towards you, and is

not so likely to see you. Remember also that it is at sun-up and sun-down that you cast the longest shadow.

Learn to move with the wind, stopping when there is a lull and continuing when it blows again. When possible, have the wind blowing from the enemy towards you, for wind carries sound, also the scent of cooking, of petrol, and so on.

Watch the animals in the fields. Sheep, when frightened, tend to huddle and look in the direction of whatever has scared them, or they run in any direction. Cows and horses will also look towards men marching, or any other unusual object or movement.

64

Watch also the wild beasts and birds. A rabbit running towards you, or past you, has been frightened by somebody else—it may be the enemy, or perhaps only another of your own men. If he runs away from you he may betray your presence to the enemy, for the woods ahead may be full of unseen foes. If birds suddenly take flight from trees and hedges, something has probably frightened them. Your movements may also frighten them and give you away, so move as smoothly as possible.

When stalking or scouting at night, remember that stillness is even more important than by day, for at night the enemy must rely chiefly upon hearing, and sounds carry better at night. If you are in open ground and it is a moon-lit night, and you think you are observed—or if a flare is dropped near you—freeze; then, when the flare dies, drop swiftly but silently to the ground and stay there motionless. If moving through cover, just stay stock-still wherever you are.

At night you should walk flat-footedly, as in the daytime, but perhaps even more slowly and deliberately. If the ground is very uneven, with hollows and rifts, it is worth feeling forward a little with the foot after you have placed it on the ground. Keep one arm extended before you so that you will feel any obstruction—a wall or hedge, bushes, underhanging branches, and so on. You may come up against a prickly hedge, and then you'll know it. Incidentally, it is well to memorize in the daytime any gaps in hedges in your area.

Crickets in the night-time may stop chirping as you pass by, thus endangering you, or if this happens in the distance it may be because of the enemy's presence. The sudden loud barking of a dog, of course, is also a danger signal.

If, with all these precautions, you or a companion make some unusual noise, never start hastily to go back. Just stop and, if you are not in cover, drop gently to the ground, and crawl to the nearest cover. If you think the enemy has scented your presence, and will come after you, you must crawl backwards, quietly and steadily, or off to the flank, unless you have the intention of risking an engagement or of luring the enemy into a trap.

Every bit of equipment you carry must be silent. Any parts which might clatter or jingle must be bound with tape or oiled, or wrapped in a rag. Use signs rather than speech, for even whispers can be heard on a quiet night. And, if you must whisper into the other fellow's ear, be careful you don't bang your tin hats together.

Stalking patrols should not be more than three or four in number. Two is a very convenient number. You must move forward at night with enough space between you to avoid bumping into each other, but not so far apart that you lose contact.

Before you go out on a job, it is important that you carefully select your line of approach, your route to your objective. This must be chosen with due regard to such matters as direction of the sun, the wind, the existence of good cover, and so on. Frequently the longer way round may be the best and the safest. And don't forget that the enemy usually has a tendency to watch the most direct route most carefully. You cannot depend upon this, of course, but, in territory unknown to him, he may not be aware of the more circuitous lines of approach. Incidentally, if you are in touch with your own troops, or other guerrilla bands, it is well to indicate to them, before starting out, what route you are going to follow, what will be the direction of your withdrawal, and, as nearly as possible, when you will start and when you will return. Always come back by another route, if possible, after you have accomplished your mission, or if observed or attacked by the enemy.

Many authorities on scouting advocate the system of "bounds" when on some form of guerrilla work in which a larger number of men is employed. If you are acquainted with the entire route, you will take note of certain objectives—buildings, copses, etc.—which mark stages in the journey. When the leader and the forward scouts reach these points, they wait for the rest of the party, under the command of another guerrilla, to catch up with them.

They plan the crossing of the next stage. This method is still more valuable when you are not well acquainted with the territory ahead of you and will therefore have to plan the route across each stage after you have gained the next point of vantage. This method cannot always be followed on dark nights.

For scouting, my favourite method of progression is the "Filibuster system," or the "staggered triangle." This calls

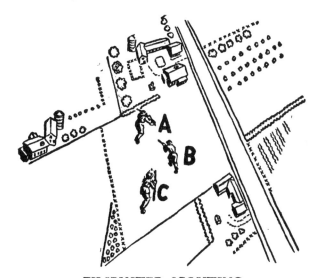

FILIBUSTER SCOUTING
When going North, C & B Protect A
When going South, A & B Protect C
When going East,   A & C Protect B

for the employment of three men who continuously remain in triangular formation, although their functions may vary from time to time.

These scouts never walk or talk together, but also they never lose sight of each other. The distance they maintain between them depends on the nature of the country; as it becomes flatter, more open, they can increase the distance between them.

This system is different from the "jump" or "bound" system, as outlined above, in which the men have to come together, every once in a while, to hold whispered conversations.

This triangle never breaks up, but the functions of the men at the three points change in accordance with the direction in which they decide to move. In advancing straight ahead, for instance, the leading scout, at the forward point of the triangle, whom we will call Number One, looks to his front, right and left. Number Two, behind him to his right, covers Number One's rear, as well as his own front and right. Number Two, of course, can equally well be to the left of Number One—the triangle can function in any direction, with its apex, Number One, always pointing in the direction in which the men are proceeding. Then, Number Three, from his place—the third point of the triangle—covers the rear of both the others against any flanking movement. If the enemy comes head-on to any of these scouts, the scouts warn their comrades by some prearranged signal. They glance over towards each other every few seconds.

Now, if the enemy were to come towards a point between Number One and Number Two, these two cross-fire, giving Number Three a chance to get away, or to come around the flank to make a diversion. If the enemy approaches between Two and Three, Two and Three will cross-fire, enabling One to get away with his information, if he has already gained any. And so on, with Two, if the enemy comes in between One and Three. The chief aim of the group is to get away without a fight if their presence is discovered.

If the triangle has to change direction, the men change their functions of leading and protecting each other. For example, if they wish to go to the right, Two becomes One, Three becomes Two and One becomes Three. If they move to the left, from the first position, Three becomes Two,

One remains One and Two becomes Three. If they retire, One and Three change functions. Each man always retains his relative position but each in turn may become leader. Each man should therefore be as good a scout as the others.

The "bounds" system is that used by the British Army and is therefore the one most likely to be taught to Home Guards. But I strongly recommend the use of the "Filibuster" system, instead of or in addition to the "bounds" system, since in my opinion it is the best suited to guerrilla warfare.

A fighting patrol will usually need more men than a patrol for reconnaissance only. In such cases the "Filibuster" system can still be used, and each point of the "staggered" triangle can consist of two, or even in some cases three, men. Or four men can adapt the system to make a "staggered square." If there is fighting to be done, and five men are available, one should be ahead, one on each flank, and one in the rear. The fifth man, the leader of the group, should not go ahead of the others, but somewhat behind the first man and to his flank.

When observing the enemy, lie flat and peer through brush or roots. Don't put your head around a bush or other cover. If you have to look over a wall, a hedge or bank, break off a branch and raise it first, then look through the leaves. A cluster of bracken or a bunch of heather will also serve. If there is a tree near the wall use it as a means of looking over.

Watch a landscape methodically for enemy movement, keeping your eyes level and watching shadows carefully. Scan a landscape methodically by definite areas.

Scouting units when they sight the enemy should send back word immediately to the commander of their guerrilla force, stating the enemy's position, whether resting or encamped or in movement, the compass point from which the group is proceeding and that towards which they are heading. Also details as to their strength, what armament they have, and so on. From this information, your commander can then decide how to deal with them, and he will send you instructions, either to retire unobserved, to wait until his party comes up to you, if desirable, or to act in such a manner as to make your presence known to them, so as to lure them into an ambush.

It is necessary for guerrillas to know how to make speedy and accurate reports. You must write clearly, using block letters if your handwriting is at all indistinct, and always printing clearly the names of places, persons, regiments and so on, also the words NO and NOT. Always use the 24-hour clock. Number every message you send back so that your commander will know if the previous one is missing. When you have put every known fact into your message—answering the questions: "What? How many? Where? When? Going where? Doing what? What weapons?"—you can draw a line and then put in your own comment as to what you think the event reported probably means. Do not mix your guess with the known facts.

If the information is very important, it may be well to send two copies of the message, by two different routes.

If you have to send a verbal message, have the messenger repeat it to you before he goes, and don't let him go until he can.

You can practise reporting, by having men carry out certain acts in front of your squad, and then getting each man to write a report, describing exactly what he has seen, not forgetting the inclusion of time, place, and so on.

Sometimes it is a help, in listening for footsteps, to stick a knife-blade or bayonet into the ground and then place your ear to it.

In the above sections, dealing with scouting, stalking, woodcraft, and so on, I have not attempted to be exhaustive, but only to indicate the lines along which you will have to study and work. There are many excellent books on these subjects, and I recommend that you examine them and practise the knowledge gained thereby.

You will, for instance, adopt some form of signalling, from one man to another. Sometimes a torch can be used;

sometimes this is not advisable, and motions of the hands or rifle are best. Adopt a simple code, and stick to it.

But one thing I would like to emphasize: Take rest whenever you can, if only for short periods. Your energy is valuable and you must conserve it. When tired and ready for sleep—naturally, only if you have no urgent task on hand—settle for rest at once. Don't wait for darkness. It is best to find your resting-place before darkness sets in. A hillside is often a good place for your night's rest. No man is likely, in war-time, to come along an open hillside. The roadside is the worst place to rest, and patrols will also probably explore ravines and valleys.

Rest whenever you can, and eat whenever you can. Even if you have eaten an hour ago, eat again if food is offered to you—you never know when you are going to eat next! But if you have been starving for a day or several days, eat any food you get very slowly. Take a few mouthfuls, then doze for a time; then eat rather more. Don't bolt food when really hungry.

Get within the enemy lines at night and hide, and lie there observing everything that goes on during the following day. Then return the next night with your information. Don't move around too much when observing the enemy. You are likely to see just as much by patiently remaining in one position, and it is much safer for you.

CHAPTER VIII

As I write this, we are being offered a supremely useful example of guerrilla tactics in the methods employed by the Russian soldiers and civilians behind the German lines. In his broadcast to these men and women Stalin expressed the objectives of guerrilla warfare. He said:

"In areas occupied by the enemy, guerrilla units . . . must be formed, diversionist troops must be organized, to combat enemy troops, to foment guerrilla warfare everywhere, to blow up bridges and roads, to damage telegraph and telephone lines, to set fire to forests, stores and transport. In the occupied regions conditions must be made unbearable for the enemy and all his accomplices. They must be hounded and annihilated at every step, and all their measures frustrated."

This expresses it in a nutshell. The Home Guard, with their elastic "web" defense system, can carry this out splendidly. Our job is to harry the enemy to such an extent that he will have to retire from outlying points to his more heavily guarded positions, and will have to devote larger and larger sections of his troops to police and guard duties, thus wasting man-power.

One of the most effective means of doing this is by the ambush. Of these there are various kinds—ambushes which are traps for the solitary motor-cyclist or car, for which a very small number—sometimes only a couple—of guerrillas is needed, and those which are designed to dispose of convoys, small bodies of troops, and so on. For the latter, larger groups must be employed.

In ambushing, three points should be borne in mind. There must be adequate cover—for the essence of ambush is surprise—you must have a good get-away arranged, and you should also decide upon a meeting-place for your group to get together again after the action, unless you already have some sort of headquarters.

It is very important to smash the enemy's communications at the first possible opportunity. This is the nerve system of his invading force upon which he is utterly dependent. It is unlikely that the Nazis will be able to use the telephone or telegraph system for some time. These will most probably be destroyed by bombardment from guns or the air, or have been put out of action before seizure by the Nazis. If they have not already been destroyed you can find innumerable opportunities for cutting telephone and telegraph wires (often tapping them first to intercept enemy messages) and cutting down the poles. You can do the same with power lines, cutting them, causing short circuits by throwing wires over high tension lines or blowing up pylons.

But most probably the enemy will have to depend on his own resources for communications for at least a period. The Nazis have developed some handy little short-wave radio transmitting sets, to get round the difficulty of communications during a *Blitzkrieg* action, but they are by no means as successful under actual fighting conditions as has been claimed. The Germans often have to depend largely on motor-cycle despatch riders.

If by any chance you obtain one of the enemy's portable short-wave radio sets, learn how to use it. Any radio engineer in your district will show you how. You can use it for intercepting enemy communications, as the Germans often do not have the time to waste on using a code. So try and have a German-speaking man in your party; he will prove invaluable on many occasions. Such radio sets can also be used to communicate with neighbouring guerrilla units if you capture more than one set. You do not need any elaborate code if you use dialect: Yorkshire, Welsh, Gaelic, etc.

My advice to guerrillas is always to attempt to stop a motor-cyclist or a private car in preference even to a tank. Holding up one message may cost the enemy twenty tanks. Strange as it may seem, with the exception of the chauffeur, a private car rarely carries a private. If you are lucky you may even land a general.

Let us suppose a small party has been told off to snare a motor-cyclist or two—but only one at a time.

A good way to stop a motor-cyclist is by stretching a quarter-inch cable or wire across a roadway. If you are sure a motor-cyclist is coming, put it up beforehand. Otherwise, have a brick tied to one end of it and be ready to sling it across the road, where others will secure it, while the Nazi is a mile away. Attach the wire to trees or fence-posts at a height of from three to three and a half feet from the ground. Don't use two posts or trees which are directly opposite each other, but, preferably, string your line diagonally across the road, at an angle of about 30 degrees. The effect of this will be to make the motorcyclist, when he hits it, slide along it and into the ditch, if there is one, or on to the verge of the road, right near where you and your companions are waiting—on each side of the road, of course, for you don't know from what direction the first rider is coming. This also leaves the roadway free for another rider who might otherwise pull up if he saw a wrecked machine lying in the middle of the highway.

As soon as your cyclist spills, go for his weapons. He is probably hurt, or busy disentangling himself from his machine. So get his weapons first and him afterwards. You will want to take him alive, although guerrilla bands have not much accommodation for prisoners. If our guerrillas have been playing Old Harry with despatch riders, the enemy may not have given him a written message, or they may have given him a fake one. Your leader will want to question him, therefore, to induce him to disclose his verbal message. And on this the lives of thousands might depend.

Even if it is impossible to take prisoners, you must capture despatch riders and question them before you "despatch" them, as silently as possible. In every case, examine the motor-cycle, and, if it is not badly damaged, fix things so that it cannot be repaired. Unless you can use it yourselves, which is unlikely unless you are in control of quite a bit of country. A motor-cycle is a noisy machine.

Always keep the enemy's weapons and ammunition. Often a guerrilla's supplies are obtained from the enemy. If you do not need them at once bury them. They may come in handy on a future occasion. It is always a good thing to examine the enemy's weapons and equipment and learn how to use them well. You never know when you may be able to use them to good account. Your own arms may wear out or be lost, then you may have to use enemy weapons.

Always thoroughly search the prisoner or the body for papers, letters, passes, etc. All these things may yield invaluable information. Identification papers may come in useful some time if you have to do a job of impersonation. Incidentally, as soon as Regulars or Home Guards take up guerrilla fighting, they must remove all badges of rank. Under guerrilla conditions they are no longer needed and are useful only to the enemy. For in the small groups used by guerrillas each officer is known intimately to his subordinates and superiors.

After an engagement be wary how you approach corpses· make certain the enemy is really dead. One man should cover the body while another examines it. One of my best friends is going round today minus an arm because a "dead man" attacked him.

Strip a dead despatch rider completely. Take away the clothes for later examination and search every inch of the body for hidden messages. Look for tattoo marks, messages hidden in the mouth, ears or other orifices. Messages may be glued to the soles of the feet. Comb the hair: look between the toes. Remember that commanding officers realize their despatch riders are riding through dangerous country, and may hide messages very cleverly. Remember also that if a despatch rider falls into your hands too easily, his messages may be fakes.

A word in season regarding this matter of uniforms. Guerrillas working in open or rough country can wear their uniforms when possible or advisable. But in densely-populated areas they will usually have to wear civilian clothes or enemy uniform. It may fall somewhat harshly on British ears to advocate the wearing of enemy uniform. But this war is not being fought according to Queensbury rules. The Nazis ignore every humane provision of warfare. They landed troops in Norway, Holland and elsewhere dressed in the uniforms of those countries, and even some dressed as women and clergymen. British stores, including uniforms, were abandoned by us in France and in Greece. So they have our uniforms, and it won't do us any harm to have theirs. And maybe guerrillas can find good use for them, once in a while!

Before we quit this question of uniforms, it is worth our while to give a thought as to how we can spot Germans who are disguised in British uniforms. If you see some British soldiers who somehow don't quite seem like British soldiers, watch them carefully, and listen hard. If you outnumber them, or if there are only one or two of them, you can talk to them, and don't forget to talk fast and slangily. They may know English fairly well, but there is a vast difference between the English they learn in school and, for instance, good rich Cockney or the bastard American which most English people have derived from the talkies. Frequently, they are unable to answer questions regarding distances, weights or measures, as they are accustomed to the metric system. Any friend of yours who has spent any time in Germany can give you tips as to how to discover whether these ostensible Britishers are Germans or not. But don't be too enthusiastic and start hammering some decent French-Canadian or one of our Czech allies!

I said, a few pages back, that privates don't ride in

private cars, or, for that matter, in military motor-cars. Their occupants—apart from the driver—are almost always officers. The enemy is bound to confiscate and use any private cars that have not been destroyed or disabled. And sometimes he may have a British civilian, male or female, driving him. In Brussels, the Germans forced Belgian women to drive their officers' cars. If you happen to be standing in a ditch or behind a tree, or some other position of safety, and you have some kind of grenade or bomb in your hand, and a car comes by with enemy officers, driven even by your best friend, you must let them have it. It is what your friend would wish you to do. And if any of the Britishers driving enemy officers are doing it willingly, all the better—it is one more Quisling the less.

Your object, in dealing with cars, is either to slow them down so that you may kill their occupants and destroy the car; or, if you have not the strength or the weapons for this, to wreck or disable the car.

It is not much good firing at a car. An ordinary rifle bullet will drill a clean hole in the windscreen, and the chances are small that you will get the driver. But an expanding "snub-nose" bullet—you can easily make one for yourself—is more likely to shatter the glass, and thus cause the driver to lose control. Then you want to let the occupants have it quick, before they can collect themselves.

A three-quarter inch steel cable, stretched at an angle rather loosely across the road between trees or fence-posts, should halt a car or a lorry.

A good car trap can be fairly easily constructed on a road which is bordered on both sides by trees. Select two heavy trees, opposite each other. At a height of three feet —if the trees grow level with the roadway; if they are on a bank, it must be lower down—peel off a foot and a half of bark from each tree, on the side facing away from the road. Then chop or saw the trees almost through, at this point, so that they will break at a moderately strong pull. Then nail the bark on again, so that no one will note the trees have been tampered with. Tie the heads of the two trees together by strong branches and attach what lumber-jacks call a "pull-away rope" with a pulley. When you tug on this, the trees will both fall across the road.

A simpler form of this trick is to use only one tree. Then the pulley is not necessary. You can also treat two trees this way, one several yards farther down the road from the other. This is a really fancy job, for then your first tree falls in front of the vehicle and the second behind it, which also obstructs any other car coming up with help. You can even stop tanks by this method, so long as the country alongside the roads is not suitable for tanks to turn into for an alternative path. In other words, if the banks at the sides of the road are very steep, if the country on either side is heavily wooded, or if on either side a hill rises sharply, or there is water or houses. But to stop heavy tanks you must fell from six to twelve trees at intervals of not more than six feet.

Incidentally—and this goes for all kinds of ambushes—never attempt to rig another ambush in the same place. And don't linger around, once the car or motor-cycle has crashed or the lorry slowed down and had a bomb whizzed into it. Your motto should always be: "Finish them! Then a quick get-away, and another ambush some place else." Most ambushes, obviously, are best laid at night—in fact, most guerrilla work is best done at night, and much of it can only be done then.

Not all roads are conveniently provided with trees for felling, or fence-posts or trees for stretching wire. If all we want is to stop or slow down a car or lorry, so that we can lob a grenade into it, this can often be accom-plished simply by placing some unusual and suspect ob-ject in the road. The enemy in a strange and recently in-vaded country is usually nervy and suspicious. A couple of children's perambulators, covered with sacking, in the road may cause them to stop—they may think it is some-thing which will go off with a bang. Even a few small branches stuck into the ground across the road, after the surface has been disturbed a bit, may make them think

ONE MAN ANTI-TANK TRENCH
(*Spanish War Type*)
Bomb or grenade bursting in centre covers all "arms."

MODIFIED FORM OF ABOVE
Overall length less. Staggering of "arms" affords greater protection.

FURTHER MODIFICATION
Still greater measure of cover. May be mistaken for some of their own
earthworks by enemy who sees Swastika sign from air.

this is some sort of land mine, and they will stop to investigate. There are innumerable devices along these lines, many of which you will be able to think out for yourselves.

And here let me say that no tactic, trick or stratagem mentioned in this book is to be applied too rigidly. Nor are those mentioned here the only ones. On the contrary, they are merely examples of hundreds, for which there is no space in these pages—and no need to write about till they are used. They are mentioned here to guide you, to stimulate you to think up other devices; and they are meant for you to use, modify, adapt, as occasion arises.

An ingenious wrecking ambush to be used at night can be made out of one or two old car headlamps and a dry battery. Rig them up so that their light will play directly into the windshield of a car or lorry coming along the road. Run the wire up from the road so that you can operate the battery from under cover. Then wait for a car to come along, and, when it does, switch on your lights when your victim is almost on top of them. The sudden glare will cause the driver to swerve and crash. This trap must be rigged just in front of a sharp turning, a steep embankment or a bridge. An advantage is that often you can rapidly take down your apparatus in the darkness (you have, of course, switched off the lights as soon as the car crashed), and use it again somewhere else. And those who examine the smash next day will be sorely puzzled as to what caused it. I have known a couple of experts who actually fixed up a gadget across the road, consisting of a flat length of metal or wood, which would operate the lights when a car passed over it. So that the guerrilla was well away when the crash came. But that is a bit too luxurious for everyday use.

Broken glass or boards pierced with nails, laid across the road, will puncture tires and hold up vehicles. To attract the closest attention of enemy car drivers or guards, prop up a good dead Nazi where they will see him.

We can also use land mines, but one does not always get the opportunity to lay these in roads. We can, however, use them before the enemy's initial advance, but then there is always a risk that they will be exploded by artillery shells or bombs from planes. You can use land mines in plenty over open ground along which infantry will pass. Bury them at night on the paths you think the enemy will follow next morning. Don't waste your land mines on small detachments of the enemy, but wait until large bodies are passing over them. If you are mining a convoy, blow up the first lorry, to make a barrier against the rest, then let your mines explode all down the line.

In ambushing tanks, many of the same rules apply as those relating to other vehicles. But a tank needs more slowing up. Either the obstruction must be bulkier, or it must be psychological. Anything which looks dangerous or puzzling might slow up a tank, unless it decided to make a crazy rush right across it. Even half a dozen soup plates, spaced across the road, can cause nervousness to the tank commander. A screen of some sort across the road, such as a blanket suspended from a rope, will make the commander think that perhaps it masks a tank-pit, an anti-tank gun or some sort of explosive trap.

Once the tanks have slowed up, the guerrillas can get after them with hand grenades or other explosive weapons.

There are grenades, as well as mines, which go off when a tank runs over them, or you have a mine or grenade attached to a string. You are on one side of the road, holding an end of the string, and your friend is on the other with the grenade. Just as the tank comes rolling along, your partner puts the grenade out on to the road and you haul on your string. While you are busy on these matters, have a couple of other men on each side of the road, of course under cover, firing at the tank with their rifles to distract the attention of its gunners.

Places where there is no negotiable country for tanks on either side of the road—woods, steep declivities or lakes, for instance—make the best places for ambushes. And also where the road takes a sharp turn. As tanks often have a motor-cyclist or two preceding them, you should have wire barriers, just round the corner, to check the motor-cyclists, and another to let down behind them when they have passed, so they cannot return to warn the tank. While your other men with their bombs are dealing with the tank, some of you open fire upon the motor-cyclists, remaining well under cover and far enough away to make the fire of the motor-cyclists' tommy-guns unreliable. Other riflemen, farther from the tank, distract its attention with their fire while those nearer the tank use their bombs. If you are strong enough to tackle a row of tanks, stop the centre and last tank, while another party deals with the first one away ahead. If you are near the side of a tank, throw your grenades under its tracks and bogie wheels. If directly in front of it—and you shouldn't be if possible—you must aim at the tank's middle, just where the turret joins the body.

Do not be overawed by tanks. They look more impregnable than they are. Don't forget that their crews tire easily under the pressure and smells inside the tank, that they have only narrow slits to see out of, and that they are almost suffocating in the hot, cramped space within. Therefore, if they think they are in relatively safe country, they travel with the top of the turret open to give a bit of air. The commander looks out of this opening, which gives him a much better view. His head then becomes a fairly good target for a rifleman. Hold your fire until the last possible moment as the tank rolls by, then let him have it. If you kill him, you may get the rest of the crew. Space is so limited inside a tank that until the crew can open the turret and dispose of the body they cannot easily manoeuvre. So be sure your first shot kills.

Attacking a closed tank with a rifle is rather like trying to kill a hippopotamus with paper darts. But there is one thing you can do. Aim at the driver's window. The glass will not break but it will star so that the driver cannot see through it. He is then forced to use the steel visor, which gives him a much more restricted field of vision. Through the slits in this visor, which are too narrow for a bullet to go straight in, bits of well-aimed bullets will splash. Rifle-fire can also knock out the periscopes through which driver or commander looks to the flank.

In ambushing enemy troops, use grenades, machine guns and rifles. One grenade skilfully plopped down into the road from a bank can do more damage than ten rifles. Support Brens or machine guns with rifle fire. Your object should be to cause confusion through surprise and then execute as many of the enemy as possible while the confusion lasts. With the first signs that the enemy is rallying, make tracks for the backwoods.

Ambush parties should always be placed so that no one loses contact with the others. The leader should be in a position to see as many of his followers as possible and to be seen by them. Some authorities advise the placing of an aiming mark to avoid firing the Brens or machine guns too high when the enemy appears. A chalk mark on a tree or wall at about the height of a man's heart will serve.

Guerrilla fighters must learn to estimate distance rapidly and accurately. You can practise this at almost any time. Let a group of guerrillas get together and estimate the number of paces between certain objects. They will write down their estimates. Then get someone to pace the distance, and the guerrilla who has guessed right, or nearest to right, gets a packet of cigarettes as a prize.

Incidentally, if you can't swim, and you are a Home Guard, or you want to be a good guerrilla fighter, start learning right now. What is a good guerrilla going to do if he comes across a river—walk a couple of miles to find a bridge? It may have an enemy sentry on it. Or waste a couple of hours trying to build a raft or steal a boat? But a log or an air-tight petrol-can will enable you to cross a river if you can swim just a little.

CHAPTER IX

AMBUSHING is not the only method of destroying the enemy's cars, lorries or tanks. The guerrilla is also adept in the practice of "invisible destruction." This means that you destroy the enemy's transport, stores, and so on, without letting him know about it until the time comes when he needs to use it. If you make a noise, or if you burn or blow up something, he may be able to catch you; also he has earlier warning of his loss, and therefore more time in which to replace it.

Of course, some forms of destruction cannot be done invisibly and silently. You cannot destroy an ammunition dump quietly. But it is better, for instance, to let petrol leak away than to burn it. If you have to blow up objects, use delayed-action bombs so that you have time to make a get-away.

For destructive raids, usually you should not have less than three men in your party. Sometimes two is better, and there are some jobs best done by one man. To do them, you may need disguises of various kinds—not false whiskers and sun-glasses, but civilian clothing, perhaps, or an enemy uniform, or women's clothes—only pick someone who can wear them naturally—or maybe a postman's uniform.

Let us say we are out to destroy a canal barge or barges. I would never try to burn it and let the enemy know for miles around that guerrillas are active. I would sink it quietly. The additional advantage of this would be that the sunken hulk might hold up traffic on the canal.

For this purpose, if it is a wooden barge, you can use a bailing-hook, such as is used by dockers to handle cargo. With this you will pull out the caulking between the planks. It may take you anything between twenty minutes

84

and two hours to pull out sufficient to sink the barge. You might also drill holes in the barge. Circumstances, and your equipment, will dictate which is preferable.

In the case of a steel barge you need a spanner to take out the draining-plug at the bottom of the barge. These methods, of course, can also be used with boats. If you can't use silent methods, blow a vessel up with a long-delayed-action bomb.

When destroying vehicles, keep an eye open always for petrol-tank lorries—to cripple or destroy them is doubly advantageous: the enemy loses the use of the vehicle, and also of the petrol.

If I succeeded in entering an enemy lorry park—almost certainly by night, of course—and had plenty of time, I would quietly remove one spark plug in each engine, then insert a quarter-inch or half-inch nut or bolt, and replace the plug. When they step on her to start her off, the next morning, the nut or bolt will smash up the motor. Or you can damage the distributor with a screwdriver.

A good trick, but a bit more elaborate, is borrowed from gangsters, who have often used it successfully to remove competitors or anti-racketeering politicians. For this you need a stick of dynamite with a detonating cap at one end to which a wire is attached. You then attach the free end of the wire to a spark plug or switch contact, and have another wire grounded to the framework of the car. When the enemy steps on his starter or turns a switch, he blows his car up and himself too.

One of the oldest sabotage tricks is to put some sand or emery dust into the bearings of a vehicle. This can also be done to railroad trains and engines.

Whenever you can drain off or destroy petrol, do so. Petrol is the life-blood of the modern army. Three or four lumps or spoonfuls of sugar put into the petrol tank, or a small bottle of linseed oil emptied into it, will immobilize any car after it has travelled three or four miles. Shredded cotton or waste, confetti, wool or sand in a petrol tank will probably block the feed-line or filter.

Some modern German tanks have a filter good enough to prevent this blocking, but their lorries do not.

Petrol draining out of a car's tank makes a splashing or trickling noise. So, if there happens to be any sand or sawdust—or perhaps a sack—around, put it underneath to deaden the sound. You can puncture petrol tanks with an awl or drill.

Tire-slashing can be done by night or day, and the guerrilla should find lots of opportunities for this, even when other jobs which take longer are impossible. Don't unscrew the air-valve from the tire, if there are people near, because the escaping air makes a protracted hissing noise. One good nine-inch slash with a strong, sharp knife along the wall of the tire-casing will let the air out in one short gasp, and will not attract so much attention.

Among the enemy's most formidable weapons are tanks. Every tank the guerrilla can destroy, or even put out of action for a time, is a minor victory for our cause. As we have seen, tanks can be ambushed by day. And the guerrilla can also go out after them at night, when they are laid up.

For tanks do have to lie up at nights. If you had ever tried riding in the hot, airless, constricted interior of a tank, you would realize that tank crews must have their rest. By night-time, they are exhausted, probably suffering from headaches, perhaps "tank-sick." They are all in.

Then is the time for you to sneak in—if the tanks are not heavily guarded by infantry—and either steal the tanks or blow them up, or throw grenades into the opened turrets.

You should be able to snaffle their sentries quietly, then go down to the lager and kill their drivers and destroy the tanks. Molotov cocktails and A.W. bombs hurled at the bogie-wheels will set the rubber on fire.

Supposing an enemy aeroplane has made a forced landing not far from your guerrilla band. Here is a heaven-sent opportunity. If it is a fighter it will have only one pilot. If a bomber, only a few men. And one or more will have to go out to make contact with his forces, to get help. At most, you will have only three or four men to overcome.

Or sometimes it may be possible to sneak into an aerodrome by night. At any rate, it is well worth while knowing how to immobilize an aeroplane. When working quietly the best plan is to attack the elevator, which is lightly made and therefore easily damaged. And it is the one control surface which renders it impossible for the plane to take the air. If you can use a little noise, plant a Mills bomb in among the instruments, tie a fishline to the pin and walk away. When you come to the end of the line, jerk the pin out.

If you have to set fire to a plane—and don't forget that this will bring the enemy down on you in a pretty short time—remember that there is bound to be petrol somewhere near the engine. Light some oil-soaked rags there. If you find a petrol tank, puncture it with any sharp object and let some of the petrol run out on to the ground. Then throw a lighted match into it, and make the quickest getaway you can, before the bombs and ammunition start popping. If you have a bomb, of course that will do the trick more quickly.

If you want to destroy an ammunition dump, or perhaps a big store of other war material, you must use a time-bomb. The same applies to a petrol dump, if you have not the time to open up the tanks with a hand-drill to let the petrol flow out.

It takes a long time to tear up railroad tracks, and the probabilities are that there will be guards posted along the line to prevent this. They can be blown up, but can usually be repaired in three or four hours. Still, this delay counts when the enemy is working to a time-schedule. It is better to blow up a railway bridge, however, if you can, as this takes much longer to repair.

Furthermore, you can blow up trains, which will also have the effect of blocking the track and wrenching rails out of place. This is an easier job, from the point of view of your get-away, because you can lay the detonators on the track, so that the train blows itself up. A slab of gun-cotton, laid on a railway metal and properly detonated, will blow a piece of the rail right out.

A land mine is good for blowing up trains, because it does not function until you want it to, if you have your wires leading from it to a position where you are pro-tected but can view the track. Then you can blow up whatever part of the train you choose, always remember-ing, if it is a passenger train, that generals usually ride in the last coach, or the last but one.

Rails unbolted and displaced will tip a train off the lines. Try this at an embankment, on a curve.

If all this is too difficult, you can still delay a train if a couple of you slither down to the track with a few gal-lons of good grease—say, axle-grease, but even smooth tar will serve—and smear the rails, always choosing a section of track which is level or up-grade. Then the pistons will be driving the engine-wheels fast, and they cannot grip the rails, and the train will be going no place fast! No engine carries enough sand to cover a long stretch of track.

Whenever there are bridges or culverts which cross rivers or streams, you have an excellent opportunity of doing some long-distance exploding. The water, of course, must have a fairly good current. Find some good cover about one hundred yards from the bridge. Float a piece of wood down stream from there, timing the period it takes to reach the bridge. Then make a tiny raft, and float that down, timing it too. Then you can make another raft on which you will place some sticks of dynamite or gelig-nite, together with a few pounds of blasting or lifting powder, with a time fuse coiled inside a can. As you have timed the current—the length of time it takes to float your raft down to the bridge—you can cut your fuse to match, so that, when the raft passes under the bridge, up she goes. This is only effective when the bridge under-surface is near the water.

There are also various types of buildings which you will

88

want to destroy, either by fire or explosives. If they contain stores, then by fire. If they contain troops, then by explosives. For this purpose, you will have to learn something about explosives, how to use them, and how to improvise bombs, hand grenades, and so on. This, I am afraid, I cannot tell you about here. But the "Explosives" article in the *Encyclopædia Britannica* will give you everything. A good deal of instruction has been given to Home

Guards in this subject—although not by any means to enough of them—so that in each guerrilla band there should be at least one person who can instruct the others in these matters. You can, for instance, make a fairly good bomb out of an empty tin can, if only you have the explosives, and know how.

No one should run away with the idea that, in performing the above destruction jobs, all we have to do is stroll quietly down to the car park, ammunition dump, or whatever it may be. We have to approach these places with infinite caution; and often we shall have to dispose of a sentry or two before we can go about our job.

Therefore we must know how to rid ourselves of a sentry's presence, silently and expeditiously. Sometimes we shall not want to kill the sentry, for then someone may find his body and give the alarm. It will not do us any harm if we now seek instruction, right in our home town, from wrestlers, ju-jitsu experts, and even doctors and bone-setters, who can show us the nerve-centres of the body, the vulnerable places, and how to control a man or put him out swiftly.

A hammer blow between a man's shoulder blades will paralyze him. If you want to take a sentry and walk him off, you must keep your left hand, with a handkerchief balled up in it, over his mouth, so that he makes no outcry. The palm or base of your hand should be pushing up under his chin, while you pinch his nose with thumb and forefinger, pulling it down. You, of course, are standing behind him. And with your other hand you are pressing your knife against his body.

Always try to take a sentry from the rear. But if you must take him from the front, never hold your gun up against his tummy, and tell him to put his hands up. Odds are he knows the trick to pull, and will get your gun before you can pull the trigger. If you do have to take him from the front, place the sole of your left foot—if you are right-handed; if not, reverse these instructions—on the arch of his right foot, pulling your revolver-hand—or knife-hand, or the hand holding whatever weapon you have chosen—as far back as possible. Then with your left hand you tear open his tunic or greatcoat, leaving the bottom button still fastened. Then grab him by the shoulder and swing him around quickly. You may slap his ears with the revolver barrel, to intimidate him. Then pull his straps, tunic, greatcoat and braces down over his shoulders to his elbows. This will lock his arms.

90

Unless you need to march him away, you should also drop his trousers to lock his feet. Then search him from head to foot—he may have a knife too.

Never tell him to put his hands up. His hands may show up on a moonlit night and attract attention; also this elongates his shadow. Besides, German sentries often carry egg-bombs, and he may have one in his hand. If you make him put his hands up you are helping him to chuck it at you. Or if he has his back to you he can throw it some distance away, to attract attention. He won't drop it if

his hands are down, for that would hurt him as much as you, and he probably doesn't care for the death-with-honour business.

Take away a sentry's pens and pencils. He may have a tear-gas gun, which looks exactly like a propelling pencil.

Practically any military or scouting manual will give you various other methods of taking sentries, so I shall not dwell on this.

But usually you will not be able to take sentries. You will just have to despatch them as quietly as possible. For this purpose, you may not be able to carry visible weapons, if you are passing through, or very close to, the enemy's lines. However, there are invisible weapons which are very efficient.

Here are some of them: Ladies' hatpins, five or six inches long. Or a wrist-knife, strapped to your wrist with the hilt downwards. A knife worn round the neck on a thong or cord. A small revolver, held up your sleeve by rubber bands or in a shoulder-holster. A stiletto with a nine-inch blade, no wider than three-quarters of an inch at its broadest, and double-edged for its full length. Be sure it has a hilt-guard on the haft. This instrument you should grasp solidly, placing the ball of the thumb along the flat of the blade. You use it with a twist of the wrist, stabbing upward and inward, under the lower rib towards the heart, or aiming at the spinal cord to sever it.

Other useful weapons are hammers—either to smash a man's skull or hit him between the shoulder-blades to stun him; cheese-cutters—the wires with wooden handles you see in the grocery stores—which are handy for strangling people; fish-lines, for strangling too, but also useful to tie a man's hands or ankles; and a handkerchief with a fistful of sand in it; and so on.

If you are going to use a knife on a man, taking him from the rear, you should keep the outside of your foot against his heel, then drag him down on to your left knee while pushing a knife between his lower ribs, or in some other vulnerable spot. Your left hand is over his mouth to prevent an outcry. Note first what vulnerable points are protected by equipment.

If ever you take a sentry, or any other enemy prisoner, with one of you covering him with a rifle, never forget the golden rule that, to search him or for any other reason, you should never pass between him and the man who is covering him. The other golden rule is: have him turn his back to you at the earliest possible moment. When he can't watch you, he can't think up tricks to take you off your guard.

Sometimes also you will blindfold a prisoner—not only

if you do not want him to see where you are taking him, but also because a blindfold prisoner is not so likely to cry out. Gags are never as good in real life as in the movies; they work loose, and a man can usually emit some sort of a yell through them.

The various methods of dealing with sentries, of course, are also useful when capturing or destroying strayed enemy soldiers, or small enemy patrols. These methods are so well known—particularly when used in connection with a rifle—that I can refer you to a dozen or more well-written handbooks, from any one of which you can learn all that I could teach. For, while these things are part of guerrilla warfare, they are also part of regular warfare.

Sometimes, when trying to get through enemy lines, you can have a companion whose job it is to distract the sentry's attention. He can quite simply toss a stone at him and make off noisily in the brush. Or you can rattle some tin cans, tied to a rope, several yards away. If in or near a town or village, a fake fight between two apparently drunken men may do the trick. Sometimes then you can whizz by the sentry or sentries in a small light car, toss your hand grenades into the factory, car park or other objective, drive on for a bit, immobilize your car, and take to the woods.

Good practice for taking sentries is the stalking game. One of you sits blindfold while the others, in turn, try to walk right up to him and touch his shoulder without his hearing their approach. As soon as he hears you, he claps his hands and you are technically dead, and the next fellow tries.

CHAPTER X

SOME of my readers will perhaps now be saying to themselves: "Well, we have been reconnoitring the enemy, ambushing him, slipping through his lines and destroying his vehicles and material. But don't we do any real fighting?"

I understand what this reader means when he refers to "real fighting"; he means a man-to-man conflict, a "shooting war."

However, what we have been studying *is* real fighting, in every sense of the word. Real fighting is anything that helps to win a war. To render useless the enemy's lorries, ambush officers in cars, destroy his petrol and wreck his trains causes far more damage than to kill a score or two of his soldiers.

But this does not mean that, if we have the chance, we shall not try to kill some of his soldiers by rifle, tommy-gun, machine-gun or Bren-gun fire. We shall jump at the opportunity—always providing that by so doing we do not "throw away a strategic advantage for a tactical gain," do not throw away our capacity to go on functioning as guerrillas.

There are many times when we shall have to fight, when discovered at our base, or when reconnoitring, or preparing an ambush.

But when we choose to fight, we must be sure that the enemy is at a disadvantage, regardless of numbers or weapons, and that he cannot get strong reinforcements before we can get away. On the battle-field we must stand up to the enemy, under any conditions; but the rules of guerrilla warfare are different. Guerrillas must live to fight another day. If absolutely cornered, of course, we guerrillas will fight to the death.

It is our job, when the enemy is on the march, or his foraging or scouting parties are out, to harass his flanks, to snipe every straggler. Hit and run. Hit and hold them up. Hit and scatter them. Select the most advantageous observation points. Arrange for your observers to warn you in good time to have traps set. Watch when and where the enemy settle down for a rest, a meal or for sleep. Surprise them by attack, both by night and day. Have your departure covered by hidden rifles and machine guns, and as you go past your comrades, make plenty of noise to lure the

94

enemy on. Then your hidden riflemen and bombardiers will go after them. Be audacious and daring. Be wise to every trick. Learn how to fix your rifle in the daytime, for night fire. Know your territory and fear nothing.

When you advance to attack the enemy, do it in systematic organized fashion. Your leader must have the whole action planned in advance, and must see that you understand it thoroughly. Sometimes you will advance on two or three different sides. You will have your scouts ahead of you, and will have prearranged signals by which they can communicate with you. The main body will proceed in one, two or three files, or will be more scattered and then converge later—it depends upon the various circumstances attending your action; I cannot give you a rigid prescription for each and any attack. Often you should move to position at night; study and get very close to your enemy during daylight; attack at dusk; get away in the dark.

When you advance to attack, your men must all arrive at their places in cover before any other step is taken. You will then be ready to fire—perhaps firing from one side only as a diversion, perhaps raking the enemy with cross-fire, right at the beginning. After the first volleys you will perhaps advance further, "belly-crawling" through your cover. Or now, perhaps, another party of your guerrillas will suddenly attack on the enemy's flank. It may be advisable for a machine gun, if you have one, or a small party of rifles, to be posted somewhere ahead and to one side, to give you covering fire until you have taken up the position from which you are best able to fire on the enemy.

Points to remember in these encounters are: never waste ammunition by firing too soon or wildly. Every shot must be aimed to kill. Be sure your man is within range, then sight him carefully and let him have it. One well-aimed shot is worth a dozen hasty ones. Make plenty of use of cross-fire. Pick off enemy officers. Have special snipers told off to get officers.

One machine gun on your right and one on your left cross-sweeping the area in front of you, will cover your whole position with a curtain of fire. When aiming at your man choose a spot in the centre of the body, about half-way between his waist-belt and the base of his throat. Don't pick a man too far to the left or right; he is probably the target of one of your companions. If possible each member of your party should pick his man. If your target is moving about don't follow him with your rifle. Instead point it a short distance ahead of him in the direction he is travelling. Hold your fire until he comes into your sights. If you see two or more of the enemy approaching cover, shoot the man nearest cover first. You can get the other later. An enemy in the open is worth two in the bush.

If you have routed the enemy and he no longer returns your fire, advance cautiously to take his arms, ammunition, uniform, etc. Don't forget he may *not* be routed, perhaps he is just playing possum.

But if he is too tough for you, withdraw. Don't panic. Retire coolly, taking advantage of every bit of cover. Some of your party should act as rearguard to fire at the enemy if he continues the pursuit. This gives time for the others to get away. It is often wise to post a machine gun or Bren in the rear to hold up your pursuers.

Way back at the beginning of this book I said that subterfuge is essential in guerrilla fighting. Unless guerrillas use subterfuge, they don't fight for long. Decoys and diversions are among the different forms of subterfuge.

Decoying is to lure the enemy on until you are in a favourable position to attack him. A diversion is a trick used to distract his attention and perhaps his fire from the point from which the attack is forthcoming.

There are so many of these, that to detail them here would require a volume you would have to carry around on a truck. Besides, every guerrilla worth his salt will invent and use new ones to fit the circumstances of the action he is undertaking. But I will mention a few, not for you to copy, necessarily, but to stimulate your own inventiveness.

Let us say that your section is way behind you in a bit

of "dead" territory. You and a companion have crawled ahead to observe the enemy. Now you are ready to act as decoys. You will expose yourselves to the enemy, at any distance from 200 to 400 yards. But only for two or three seconds at a time and, of course, each time at a different point.

The best rifleman in the world could not throw his rifle to the shoulder, allow for windage, elevation and distance, and shoot you during these few seconds. And if he takes a snap shot, it is merely a waste of ammunition. The tommy-gun, at such ranges, is not too accurate.

Then get down and work back towards your companions, taking every advantage of cover. But every now and again, you will "inadvertently" expose yourself again. Don't do it too obviously, or they will scent a trap. You are the bait—and they the fish. If you have to, you can shoot back, when you are "discovered." Don't shoot the first man down, aim for the last, or the others will try to outflank you. It will be only you and your partner against a score or so, so your firing won't really stop them; and eventually you will have lured them into the trap.

Verey lights are useful by day and by night. If you fire off a couple in the daytime you will find that they will halt advancing enemy troops. The enemy will probably send out patrols to discover what it is all about, thinking they are signals of some sort. Don't send up any lights then for a while.

But just as soon as the main body again starts to move, send up a couple more Verey lights. Again the enemy may send out scouts, who will probably advance with less caution than before, thinking perhaps that this is just a stunt to hold them up.

By the second time the scouts have returned and the enemy starts to move again, your Verey lights will go up once more. Now the enemy will be sure this is only a trick to hold them up and they will continue onward. Then strike them from the flanks and the rear. They will probably be afraid to go forward into the unknown and will either make a stand or fight back to where they were.

Nazi parachutists sometimes use Verey lights as rallying signals; their fighting patrols use them as success signals. When they do so, use them yourselves to mislead them.

Another ruse is to put up a fairly weak fire, right in front of the enemy, so that they imagine they have an easy opponent to deal with, and will advance with confidence. In the meantime, the two main sections of your band have been lying concealed on either flank of the enemy. When he advances, they will converge on his rear and attack him.

A few of you, providing you have adequate cover, can manœuvre the enemy into a position in which you can attack him with advantage. What you have to do is to convey the impression that there are many of you, attempting to close in on him. You must move rapidly from one part of the cover to the other, occasionally showing a helmet or rifle barrel above the cover, and taking pot shots at the enemy from various angles.

Some beleaguered Russian guerrillas, during the Civil War, had to light fires under their machine guns, in the midst of winter. But, if they had only three guns, they would light a dozen fires, and move the guns from fire to fire to mislead the enemy as to the number of their guns, and their position.

If you are attacking an enemy who is hiding in a wood, post sentries around the wood so that each is at visual distance from his neighbours on either side. Then quarter off a section of the wood and machine-gun it thoroughly. When this is done, you can advance your sentries through this section, thus narrowing the guarded area. Then machine-gun the next outer section of the wood, and so on, bringing up your sentries each time. When beating a wood, your grenade-throwers should advance behind the beaters, to be called up when needed. However, men in the beaters' line can carry light anti-personnel bombs, as these throw no fragments back to injure the beaters. You can also toss smoke-generators into the woods, and the coughing will soon reveal the enemy. If it is the right time of year, you can set fire to the woods. This is also one time when bayonets are handy, for they can be used to probe thickets or brush. Pitchforks are good for this too, and also for searching haystacks.

Numerous, also, are the methods of diversion. I remember how, in Mexico, where I did some fighting after the

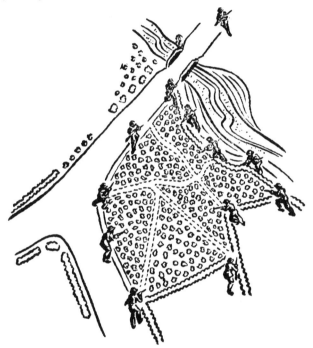

World War was over, one of our men had to get through the enemy lines with a message. While the messenger crouched ready to go, his companion, at some little distance, tied a mouse-trap to a tree with a couple of yards of stout line. When the other man was ready to run, his comrade inserted a cat's tail in the mouse-trap and snapped it to, and then ran for all he was worth. The cat dashed to and fro, screaming, and the sentry came to investigate, while the messenger crawled through the lines. It was tough on the cat, but it got the goods.

At night, to divert enemy sentries or scouts, it is not a bad idea to imitate the hooting of an owl so atrociously badly that they know it is not an owl. Their attention will be centred on the spot from which came the hooting, while another of your men does his dirty work farther along the line. You can also whistle fake signals to each other; and so on.

A classical example of subterfuge is one employed when I was serving with the forces of General Sandino, in Nicaragua. I was with a party of Sandino's men which had been chased by night by the Federals up a donkey-path which meandered up a steep mountainside, amidst heavy thickets of thorny bush. Having no machetes to cut the bush away, we just had to keep on climbing.

Eventually we came to a little plateau and clearing, where there were a few huts. In front of one was a can of luminous paint. What it was doing there, we never knew. There was also a goat tethered to a stake. We seized the paint-brush and gave the goat a thick coating of the evil-smelling phosphorus paint; and then, with a hearty but not malicious kick, sent the old fellow careering down the mountain path. Just how effectual this stratagem was I cannot say, for we did not stay to find out. But it must have sufficiently delayed our pursuers, for we made a clean getaway.

Haystacks make beautiful bonfires at night, for a diversion, or if you need light to observe the enemy's position for an attack. And, by setting them on fire, we are implementing the "scorched earth" policy so excellently followed by the Russians.

If an enemy plane flies over you, keep absolutely still. Do not raise your faces; they show up. If it is a fighter, it may be out scouting to locate guerrilla bands. If you are in the open and there is no cover when a plane is sighted, your leader should give the word to scatter. Never bunch up.

Those who can find protection standing up should do so, behind trees, hedges, buildings, and so on, rather than move while the pilot sees you. Those who can get in a kneeling position should do so; and those who find shelter best lying down will do that. It all depends on the kind of cover you are nearest to.

But there are occasions when the plane has spotted you and is going to bomb or machine-gun you. Then hit back, if there are plenty of you, by means of "controlled firing." You divide into, say, three sections. Each section fires in unison in its turn so many lengths ahead of the plane, making three distinct fields of fire through which the plane must fly, each firing one plane's length ahead for each 100 yards distance away. If it is in a deep dive, all fire at once at its descending nose.

Never let planes distract your attention from oncoming tanks. That is sometimes the object of their attack.

For all these tactics, stratagems and actions, you will need a system of signalling. Or, rather, you will probably adopt several systems, each to be used according to circumstances.

Sometimes you will use the regular army system of hand signals. Sometimes you will use torches, which can be used both by day and night. A bright or red-covered torch fixed high up in a tree, carefully pointed the right way, can be used by day to signal to your observation post. A blue torch can be used at night; if the enemy sees it, he will not be sure what it is. Half a dozen combinations of flashes and dashes are sufficient to meet most emergencies. Sometimes you can use the time-honoured method of imitating bird-calls, but remember to imitate those which are seasonable. Find out what calls are heard most often around you, and use those. But do them well, or not at all. Under some circumstances, whistles can be used. Sometimes you can use the "Indian blanket system," which was practised by the Redskins in America. This is done by placing fires where your observers can see them—and, to the best of your knowledge, where no one else can. Then you stand by the fire with a blanket and alternately obscure and reveal the fire, according to a prearranged system of dots and dashes. If you know the Morse Code—and it won't do a guerrilla any harm whatever to learn it—you can send any kind of message. But these fires should not be left to burn long. Better to change your position and light another one than to use one too long.

Arrange with village women to do their real cooking at unusual hours. At normal cooking hours, thick smoke from certain chimneys will convey to you messages or warnings.

If guerrillas happen to know the system of semaphore signalling, they can talk to each other without waving their hands above their heads, by signalling short-arm, with the elbows down. You have only to watch a couple of Navy signalmen talking to each other in a pub by this means to know how it's done.

People attending my lectures sometimes ask me for a detailed list of the equipment of a guerrilla fighter. It is hard to describe the equipment which will serve for all times and all occasions. It depends on where you are and what job you are doing.

If you are working within a town or city, you will simply take with you that which is necessary for the particular act of sabotage or other action you are contemplating. It may just be a bomb, and a revolver to shoot your way out of trouble, if need arises.

But when the guerrilla is fighting and living in open country, he must have the equipment to keep going as a soldier. If, for instance, he is acting as a scout, and may be out alone, or with only a couple of companions, for several days, he should have the following equipment.

First of all, money. Commanders must always make sure, when their men go out on guerrilla work, that they are provided with a fair amount of ready cash. Money can often buy you out of trouble. It can buy you information, or a change of clothes. If the commander has no money, he can always get some from the bank—if there's any left there. It will be a race between you and the Germans who gets it first. If your local banker is in the Home Guard, he should give the officers a hint as to how they should effect an entrance, if ever the area is occupied; and he can give them the safe combinations when the enemy invades.

The rest of the equipment is as follows:

FISH-LINE, 25 to 30 yards long.
SMALL BLACK TORCH WITH BLUE LENS (blue blends with the night, while still bright enough for signals).
REVOLVER.
BINOCULARS, if possible adaptable to night-watching.
RIFLE, WITH BAYONET.
COMPASS.
WATER BOTTLE.
GOOD NINE-INCH KNIFE.
BURNT CORK, for camouflaging face and hands.
PHOSPHORUS MATCHES, can be used as ordinary matches and also, if wetted and rubbed on rear end of the foresight of a rifle, will help you to aim more accurately in the dark.
ONE GROUND SHEET, can also be used for camouflage.
ONE BLANKET, dark in colour—or it soon will be!
ONE (AT LEAST) 36 HAND GRENADE OF MILLS BOMB.
SPARE PAIR OF DARK WOOLLEN SOCKS, and heavy extra-large pair to pull over shoes.
PIECE OF SOAP, to keep feet in good condition if for no other purpose.

Wear woollen clothes; they are better for you if you are exposed to damp and cold, and also they don't make swishing noises when you are moving about through undergrowth.

Carry no personal letters with you. Your pass or identification papers must not give you away as a guerrilla.

The fish-line is particularly useful. It can be used to tie a captured enemy's hands or ankles. Tied to a piece of dead wood or a tin can, and with the line stretched at full length from you it can be used as a diversion. You can set a trap with it, by placing your grenade in a bush and pulling the pin half out. Tie the fish-line to the pin and the other end to a tree, three or four inches above the ground. If an enemy comes along he will trip the line and explode the grenade. Make sure you are at least 50 yards away from this booby-trap. This can be used to warn you, when you are asleep, if an enemy is approaching. Only see to it that your sleeping place has only the one approach. You cannot risk this if the woods are fairly full of your own men.

Also, if you wish to sleep guarded, you can tie the line to bushes or trees in a circle around you, with one end round your wrist; or with a couple of tin cans tied on to it to jingle when someone comes near. It is remarkable how empty tin cans abound in the English countryside, even at its wildest.

If you want to hide your equipment, tie it up in the fish-line and drop it down a hollow tree, or in a river or stream, leaving the end of the line protruding so that you can pull it up again.

Sometimes it is well to add an axe to your equipment, and, for some purposes, digging or entrenching tools are necessary.

A few simple first aid necessities—bandage, iodine, and so on—will also be useful.

Then there is the question of food. A quarter of a pound of raisins and a quarter pound of chocolate makes a splendid iron ration, which will keep you going for a week if you are sparing with it and can't get anything else. If possible, make it unsweetened chocolate which doesn't make you so thirsty. However, raisins and chocolate are not too easy to obtain, I know. So you may have to use that ubiquitous fish-line of yours to snare birds or rabbits, or to fish with. Your torch is even better for fishing, if you wade into a shallow stream and hold the torch just below the surface. Fish are attracted by light, and when they come close to it you can grab them or stab them with your knife. Birds can also be dazed at night by torchlight, so that you can knock them off their perches with a stick.

For vegetables, you have the farmers' fields, if they have left anything in them. You can sometimes send men to town to buy food. And there are the folk of the countryside and the towns whom you know are trustworthy, and who will not refuse food to a guerrilla fighter, although, for their own sake, it is sometimes better to take it apparently by force or theft.

CHAPTER XI

GREAT BRITAIN is one of the most densely populated countries in the world. Apart from the moorlands, the Highlands of Scotland, and one or two other exceptional areas, every hiker knows that you cannot walk 20 miles in this country without coming across villages and towns.

Yet there are so-called military experts who seem to envisage fighting in this country as taking place solely in rural country. We potential guerrillas are not making the same mistake. We know, as Mr. Winston Churchill has said, we shall have to fight in every street and every house, when and if the enemy lands.

Therefore we must train our Home Guard, and all who desire to participate in guerrilla fighting, in the specific tactics of street fighting. Street fighting is not a negligible episode in a modern war; it is a very important factor. Towns may be made into fortresses, and may hold up the enemy for long periods, as the experiences of Madrid, in the Spanish war, of Warsaw in Poland, of Leningrad in Russia have shown. In the resistance of the Russian people to aggression, we have seen how towns and villages, stoutly and skilfully defended by regular or guerrilla forces, can be quite literally thorns in the flesh of an advancing enemy. A town can be the centre of a defended area, as at Tobruk, that holds up the enemy indefinitely.

Casualties are always very high in street fighting, but

105

the advantage is invariably with the defenders. Ordinary dwelling houses or commercial buildings form excellent cover, and, if the town has previously been bombed or shelled, the demolished buildings, with their great piles of rubble, and heavy beams or steel girders, are still better.

Enemy tanks can do very little in street fighting. Nor for that matter can the enemy's artillery or dive bombers help in actual street fighting, for, once the enemy has entered a town, their shells or bombs are likely to cause as much harm to their own troops as to the defenders.

While a tank can smash through one or two flimsy cottages, it cannot plough along, over or under rows of houses. In a city or town it has to keep to the comparatively narrow streets, and this means that it can be held up by easily constructed barriers. One overturned tram-car, or a couple of earth-filled lorries, may stop tanks. Furthermore, tanks in cities can be effectively fought by anti-tank grenades flung from roofs or windows—windows high enough for you to be well out of range of the tanks' guns. Or grenades can be thrown from areas and basement windows, or from cellar or sewer man-holes under which a packing-case or chair has been placed for the defender to clamber up on when he gets the chance to fling a grenade under a passing tank.

On the other hand, it is very easy for anyone with a machine gun to command a straight stretch of street, or a street-crossing. For this reason, a good deal of street fighting—progressing from street to street, or occupying and fortifying fresh buildings to use as strong points—is carried on at night. Though the enemy is quite near you—they may be in the adjoining street, or even on the other side of the same street—they don't know what you are doing.

The weapons you will find most useful in street fighting are tommy-guns, which—as gangsters and G-men have taught us—are ideal for city work; revolvers, pistols, Mills bombs, anti-tank grenades and any kind of "pocket artillery." Rifles are useful, usually as snipers' weapons, although rather an encumbrance when clambering over roofs or garden walls. Within buildings bayonets are far more trouble than they are worth. Just try, if you like, half a dozen of you running up and down stairs and in and out of rooms with rifles with fixed bayonets—you'll probably do more damage to the men on your own side than to the enemy, apart from getting them caught in curtains, furniture, and so on. If you want to despatch an enemy quietly use a dagger or some kind of "cosh."

Other equipment for street fighting includes torches, candles—quite probably the electricity supply will have failed—smoke bombs—for cover when crossing streets, etc. —and barbed wire. If you cannot get army smoke generators, you can make smoke cover for yourselves out of cotton waste soaked in oil, straw, dry dung mixed with gunpowder, pitch and tar.

For house-to-house work—this doesn't mean canvassing, as we shall see further on—you will also need a pickaxe, trenching tool or crowbar. An axe is also very handy. And have plenty of filled sandbags.

To convert a village or town into a fortress you will need to erect serviceable barricades. Old and unusable motor-cars or lorries, filled with sand or loose earth, are very good for this purpose, as they can be wheeled into place at a moment's notice. Have them already loaded in readiness. You must turn the vehicle over when it is in place, and take the wheels off. You will find a strong rope, fixed to the car's axle or chassis, and brought up over its top, will help your efforts to tip it over. Or a large tree, growing by the side of the street, can be sawn nearly through and pulled across the road when a block is needed.

Flimsy barricades of the traditional kind, such as we see in illustrations of the French Revolution or the Commune, made of furniture and mattresses, etc., are of no use against modern arms and tanks. Their sole utility might be as a temporary shield to enable you to cut across the street, protected from view. If an enemy machine gun is already in place, you will not get the chance to build such a barricade.

Nor will you ever defend barricades in the old traditional manner. It is too easy for the enemy to lob bombs over them from their mortars, or even to throw grenades over them. Barricades can be defended, but by covering fire from houses, piles of debris, and so on.

Barbed wire is also useful in streets for holding up motor-cyclists and infantrymen, and it has the advantage that it can be rapidly adjusted. But it must not be used stingily.

Before the enemy attacks a town, he will shell and bomb it. The second his bombardment is lifted, his trained units will speed into the town. You must be ready. Therefore, take shelter from his shells and bombs in places which you can use later advantageously to repel his attack. Such places, affording good shelter, are concrete blockhouses and Anderson shelters placed inside the rooms of fortified houses. The blockhouses and fortified houses must be chosen so that they face each other across the street and have a good field of fire, and can also cover each other.

While you stay in buildings, you are protected, but as soon as you go out on to the open street you are at the mercy of machine-gun fire. Therefore get your men across the street in the night-time if you can. If, however, you cannot wait, provide them with a smoke screen. Even if a machine gun has a fixed alignment on the street, the gunner will have to keep firing continuously as he does not know at what moment you may be crossing in the smoke. This will overheat the barrel of his gun. When he stops to change it, dash across. Learn the firing rhythm of enemy machine guns, the pauses between bursts, the longer pauses when belts or magazines are empty.

An emergency screen can be obtained by slinging one or more blankets across the street from upper windows, attached to wire or ropes. Wet the blanket first to make it heavier. A rug can be used. Then throw a weight attached to a string across from one window to the other.

108

Then the men catching the weight can pull over the rope with the blanket on it which has been connected to the string. A machine gun cannot keep firing continuously, and your men can dash across behind the blanket screen during the pauses. The screen can also be used to mask the hurried movement of a small body of men up or down the street.

In proceeding along a street—if you must use the street —walk on the right-hand side, keeping close to the houses. The riflemen in the houses on the right can hardly see you, much less get a good aim with their rifles. The enemy in the houses on the other side have to hold their rifles in a most awkward position to sight you, unless they can shoot left-handed.

Let me strongly advise all guerrilla fighters to practise shooting left-handed, and from other awkward positions, such as tree-tops. Left-handed men should practise right-handed shooting. You will find this is not time wasted. Remember how many good shots in billiards you have to pass up, if you can't switch the cue over to your left hand!

The crowbar or pick is used for house-to-house work. The safest, and in the end quickest way of working your way down a street in street-fighting is the "house-hole method" of moving through the houses by knocking holes in the party-walls. This is the best method for either attack or defence, giving you far more mobility of fire as you can shift machine guns and rifles from house to house unobserved. It also provides a safe get-away. You avoid the dangerous necessity of moving along the open street.

In the Spanish Civil War, notably on the outskirts of Madrid and in Belchite, the mouse-hole system proved very effective for attack on a street which the enemy had captured.

Entrance to the first house is gained by letting off a smoke bomb (if you have one) and then creeping up to the front or back door and blowing the lock out with a hand-grenade. (Beware of the booby-traps as you enter.)

Once in the house strengthen the smashed door; then

109

allocate some of your men to search the house and make a fortified room on the ground or first floor. In the meantime the other members of the party should make a mousehole in the wall between your house and the next. Work fast but coolly, keeping well to one side of the hole in case the enemy fires through it. As soon as the hole is large enough, throw a grenade through to kill any occupants of the room. If you think one is not enough, slip another couple through until you feel fairly certain they are all killed. Then enlarge the hole and go into the next house, using every precaution. You can even use the time-

honoured stunt of sticking a hat or helmet through the hole first.

If the Germans attack you in this mouse-hole way, occupy the room above, and the rooms around, the room into which they will break. Stretch trip-wires if you have time. Make loop-holes into the "battle-field" room and fire low.

As you progress along a street by the house-to-house method, leave three or more men in each to occupy a room or floor from which they can keep up a heavy fire to suggest the presence of a considerable force (if they have the ammunition). If you are going to occupy these houses for some time, your little garrison should fortify their rooms, cutting loop-holes.

Progress only along one side of the street, as the enemy may be in occupation of the other side, and therefore his planes and artillery will be chary of bombing the street. Some sort of sign should be prearranged by which your own men can tell when a house has been occupied by your forces—something not conspicuous, such as a piece of rag in an upper window.

As you mouse-hole along one side of a street, you can deal with enemy-occupied houses on the other side by directing three converging lines of fire on each opposite house in turn. This fire will come from the house directly opposite the enemy house, and from houses up and down the street from it. When one opposite house is put out of action, you may be able to dash across to take it; then you can mouse-hole along, once you have taken the first house, to drive the enemy out of other houses.

Mouse-holes are also useful in attic party-walls of houses, not for attacking but for rapid movement and for observation. A few tiles displaced in the gables will give you an excellent observation post.

It is not always possible to use the mouse-hole method of taking a street. When this is the case, employ the following method. Divide into two parties, each on one side of the street, starting at the street's beginning and covered by the sides of the first houses. Each party then directs a diagonal cross-fire, with machine guns, rifles and rifles with cup-discharger attachments for lobbing grenades, at the first house on the other side of the street.

Say that Party Number One, on the left-hand side, has put the enemy out of action in the first house on the right-hand side. Number Two party will then make a quick dash, under cover of Number One's cross-street fire, into the house. From here, they open fire across the street until the first house on the left-hand side is ready for party Number One's occupancy. The two parties then direct their fire—always diagonally—at the two next houses on the right and left respectively, until they too are ready for occupation. And so on, right up the street. The diagram will make this method clear. This method would have to be used, for example, in a street of detached or semi-detached houses, where mouse-holing is impossible.

Always note possible get-aways in houses you occupy,

such as back windows, negotiable garden-walls. Sometimes roofs provide a good means for unobserved movement.

Many detached or semi-detached houses have a "blind side," a side with no windows, or just one or two small bathroom or toilet windows. We can use this side to climb up on to the roof with the aid of a rope and grappling-hook. A grenade down the chimneys will surprise enemy occupants.

Once your party is inside, they should search the house. Make as little noise as possible. Never blunder into a room, but use the utmost caution. Opening a door may explode a booby-trap, or there may be enemies in the room, just as quiet as you are, waiting for you to poke your head round the door. Poke a helmet round the door, if you like, and he *may* take a shot at it, although he prob-ably knows the trick as well as you do. However, it cannot do any harm. If you think there is someone in the room, toss a grenade into it—that will probably settle him.

When men are searching a house, others should never wait in the hallway. This is the most vulnerable spot in the house—anyone upstairs can drop a bomb down on top of you.

It is safest to search a house from top to bottom; when you can, get across the roofs and get in through a skylight, gable window or a hole in the roof.

Once you hold a house, strengthen it. This is particu-larly important if you want to convert a building into a real "strong point." This should be a house which com-mands approaches to several points from which the enemy may attack, in which case you will fortify an entire floor, so that you can keep a look-out and fire in all directions.

Once you are installed, sandbag the windows, if pos-sible. If not, use heavy furniture and mattresses piled up in front of them, to keep out hand-grenades as well as rifle bullets. Not only the windows of your strong room but those of other floors should also be fortified, for the enemy can always throw a grenade through them.

Then you must make your loop-holes for observation and firing. If you remove a couple of bricks you will have a fairly good loop-hole. Make more loop-holes than you need—the others, perhaps larger and a bit more obvious, are for the enemy to fire at. Have your loop-holes at vari-ous levels. Hang or prop mattresses, sandbags or folded blankets a few feet behind the loop-holes to stop enemy bullets ricocheting. If part of the outer wall is covered with thick creeper, this is a good place to make one of the loop-holes you really intend to use. When covering a window with sandbags, you can leave a few chinks open between the bags—fix this with strips of wood, if necessary —for observation holes.

Don't forget to barricade heavily the downstairs doors against hand-grenades. And always have your get-away either from the back, over the roof, into another house, or even, if you have had the time to make it, a shallow "crawl-trench" running through the garden.

If you know your sewer system thoroughly—and you should see to it that you do—you may be able to transport troops rapidly behind the enemy lines in a city, in order to surprise him. But look out for the fumes from damaged gas mains as well as sewer gas—your respirators are no protection against that. In London or Glasgow, the underground railway system can be used to move troops rapidly.

Previous knowledge of the territory is tremendously valuable in street-fighting. The man who knows the ins and outs of the town can always keep the enemy guessing. If you dive down a man-hole, you should know where the conduit leads to; you will know which particular backyard backs on to such-and-such an alley, and which doesn't. You know which walls and fences are low enough for you noiselessly to lift a push-bike over them and pedal away. You will know just where a 20-ft. plank or ladder can be extended from one top-storey window to another as a foot-bridge. Also where ladders are kept, and ropes.

If you have to retire, vacate three or four houses. Set the first one on fire to act as a barrier between you and them. In the next ones you can exercise your schoolboy malice and ingenuity in setting booby-traps, only instead of buckets of water use bombs. Besides delayed-action bombs planted in hiding-places, hang Mills bombs on doors so that they explode when the doors are opened. Put one in the refrigerator, so that when the enemy comes scouting for food he gets a bellyful.

Don't forget when you fortify your room to bring vessels of water into it both for drinking and extinguishing fires.

114

When attacking a town by the house-to-house method, plan the whole action ahead of time. Don't just choose any old street. Get a plan of the town and decide to occupy streets which converge on the enemy's position. As your men progress along the streets, they can break out sideways to meet each other, so that your occupation spreads gradually with the detachments coalescing like blots upon paper which spread until they meet.

CHAPTER XII

MOST of what I have written about in the preceding chapter consists of "ordinary" street-fighting, which is carried out by any troops, not necessarily guerrillas.

Guerrillas in a town, who are not numerous enough to do all the jobs I have been describing, can still be a great nuisance to enemy forces in occupation. The easiest way to do the job is to use the roofs.

A sniper on a roof-top looks down the street towards a building the Nazis have taken as headquarters. He waits until an officer comes out. If he is a good sniper the officer stays there on the pavement; and the first Nazi soldier who starts shooting back stays there too.

After a bit the Nazi will get to the door of the building, on the roof of which he is working. The sniper has a private way out, across a roof, then perhaps through an attic, into some building quite a long way away.

The guerrilla in a building or on a roof must be patient, and may have to take position before dawn. He should cover himself with sacks. He should not be tempted to fire before he has a perfect target. He should be lying so far back that his rifle cannot easily be seen. And he must judge wisely the moment for his get-away.

In cities guerrillas can get the co-operation of the local population in a way that is impossible in the country. In rural areas guerrillas depend largely on people acting individually to aid them, or protection and aid from a number of individuals in a small village. In such cases the majority of these people have been tipped off in advance just what they are supposed to do to help. But in cities you can get mass aid from thousands of people, who will do the right thing at the right moment even though not more than one or two out of a thousand people have been "in on" your plans. How is such "spontaneous" action possible?

The first step is to make large numbers of people aware that you exist. This is done by illegal leaflets, newspapers, radio, word of mouth. The best people to spread the news for you are shopkeepers, delivery boys, doctors, visiting nurses, plumbers, postmen: anyone in distributive or service work. The Nazis must allow some of the local population to do such work; so many people are needed. They cannot hope to get more than a handful of Quislings for such jobs. This method is as old as history: the proverbial place for secret messages being the inside of a loaf of bread. In the old days this was one of the few articles which most householders in a town bought daily and did not make at home. But today our opportunities are much greater; many more things are obtained from the local shops, which means all the more means of communication are open to you. You don't have to try and get word directly into every household; your leaflets only need get to a tiny proportion of the population. They will do the rest: rumour is a powerful thing.

Once you have given people hope, told them that champions exist who will show them how to fight Nazi occupation, they will wait eagerly for something to happen and hope for a chance to join in.

One of the best ways to start is to give a city a good laugh at the expense of the Nazis. Yes, I'm serious. You'd be surprised how a good laugh will give people courage and hope. The Austrian Socialists, in that invincibly gay city Vienna, have shown us the way: they developed a devastating technique against the Austrian Fascists. One night the whole of Vienna was placarded with a most official-looking poster which read: "MUNICIPAL POLICE FORCE OF VIENNA—NOTICE. Owing to the large number of political arrests which the Police must make during these troubled times, they have not enough time to deal with ordinary criminals. We therefore appeal to the loyal citizens of Vienna to co-operate with us by dealing with petty thieves, burglars, etc., themselves. We feel sure you will be glad to help us in this emergency, leaving us free to deal with really dangerous criminals."

That technique can be used very effectively to cause all sorts of dislocation. Placard the town with a notice: "Mothers desiring extra milk for their children should apply to the Town Hall within the next three days." Then sit back and watch the fun. The ensuing "riot" will dislocate the bureaucratic machinery for days. And the women won't be angry with you. They'll soon tumble to what you're up to, and the next time you start something many will cooperate actively instead of unconsciously.

It is even possible to get a courageous man to pretend he is a "loyal" civil servant, and from his position he can smuggle false official announcements in among the real ones. One Austrian not only did that, but acted his part so well that he was put in charge of the investigation to discover the criminal.

When dealing with guerrillas in general we suggested that their objective was the enemy's material, then his morale, and then the actual lives of his men. There is another objective for city guerrillas: the intangible thing called organization. City life is a complex web of services and intercommunication, that spreads out from the city to the whole of a country. Dislocation is the aim: the old story of a nail missing in a horse's shoe, therefore the shoe came off, therefore the horse went lame, therefore the general's message was late, therefore the battle was lost—that child's tale can be repeated in a dozen different forms in a city. The electric light goes out just when it is needed, and that failure may affect the issue of fighting 300 miles from the city. Belgrade's telephones cease to work, and therefore guerrillas can seize a large area in Serbia. Street gutters are blocked up, and when the rains come streets are flooded. These things do not necessarily destroy material or hit at men; they destroy organization, and thereby weaken the enemy more than if a certain amount of material was destroyed.

The "V" campaign has shown how much can be done to link and unite the forces of those who are necessarily working under cover.

Other jobs can be done on a smaller scale. Get two women to start a bread or egg riot down one street, to distract the police and guards while you are doing a useful job of blowing something up round the corner. Factory workers will start a fight or other distraction while you are doing a bit of sabotage in the next room. They will also smuggle out of factories material—metal, explosives, etc.—which you need for your work. Impersonate a high German official and walk into a factory and give orders that will tangle things up for weeks.

On all these jobs in cities women are often your best "undercover" workers. They can always think up excuses that will puzzle any man. They know how to act "dumb" when useful; they've been doing that all their lives with "Darling, how clever you are!" So use mainly women for your intelligence work and communication. A guerrilla blesses a woman's tongue, whether gossiping (really passing a vital message) or shrilly screaming at a German soldier or policeman. And as for a mob of angry women, what man can face that?

Women will gladly organize food supplies for guerrillas working outside a city; arrange for hospital care for your wounded and safe hide-outs where you can hold Staff conferences.

Don't forget small boys. For once their devilish ingenuity can be put to some good purpose.

You may be worried about reprisals against the civil

118

population. It is a nasty problem. One thing is certain: the Nazis will terrorize the population in any case. When guerrillas first show their hand the situation will get worse. But if you play your cards right, they will soon find that terror doesn't work; it makes people get even more out of hand. If it is ever possible to capture and hold some Germans as hostages, do so. Hostages can be used to stop some reprisals.

City guerrillas can be even more invisible than any others. You can work through so many thousands of people that it is well-nigh impossible to trace the origin of any "spot of trouble." Make them feel you as an impalpable presence, until every ordinary pedestrian seems likely to be a guerrilla in disguise. Soon the conquerors will be the people who are "terrorized." Above all, you must wreak immediate vengeance on any British "rat." Quislings are usually cowards; you must make them feel that they have more to fear from you than the Nazis. The patriots in Norway, China, Czechoslovakia, Yugoslavia, etc., all know that, and "bump off" these tools of the conqueror at every opportunity.

Guerrillas are always "on the run," so they must have as many hide-outs as possible. Sometimes it will not be possible to choose a known hide-out. You will be surprised how often perfect strangers will take extraordinary risks to help you, but in turn you must make it as easy for them as possible, while at the same time taking precautions against betrayal. This is how you should go about this ticklish business.

In war-time, when the invader is among us, people are hesitant about opening their doors when strangers call. So you should have as many people as possible in the district know you by sight. Find out the doctor's address. Then you can tap on the door and say, "Doctor, Mrs. Smith is ill." He will open up and you can enter. If Mrs. Snooks' daughter is being courted by Jimmie White, you knock on the door and say, "Mrs. Snooks, I've got a message for Sally from Jimmie White." The door opens and in you go.

When you do go in, keep your face covered, either with a mask, handkerchief or burnt cork. If they don't recognize you, they can't give you away, even under the severest pressure. If they know your voice, a coin or pebble under your tongue will help disguise it. This may sound melodramatic, but it is worth doing.

Once you are in the house, tie them up and gag them, and put them down in the basement or somewhere else out of harm's way. They cannot then be accused of harbouring you unwillingly. And, perhaps, they are indeed harbouring you unwillingly—there are always weaklings among us, and even a few Nazi-lovers, here and there, who have not been sent to gaol.

Always leave some money on the table, to pay for what you have used. And, if it is safe to do so, you can notify someone by phone—if it's working, although it shouldn't be with you fellows around the town—from a public callbox to go and release them.

The life of a guerrilla fighter is exhausting—physically, mentally and nervously—lonely, perilous, hard in every way. The guerrilla must sometimes work in isolation, must lurk in the shadows and take terrifying risks in broad daylight. Yet throughout all the history of warfare men ready to struggle for the freedom of their country have taken those risks. The men of today are not less capable or courageous than those of the past. Women and youngsters are just as able as in the past to show reserves of courage, even of audacity. Whether it is here in Britain, resisting invasion, or whether it is in Europe that the guerrillas of today and tomorrow will be working, they will do as well as the guerrillas who helped to defeat the Plantagenets in Scotland or Napoleon in Spain. I hope that the hints and tips in this book may be of service to them.

PENGUIN BOOKS

Fiction and Non-Fiction

Here is an excellent selection of first-rate Penguins that will satisfy the most discriminating reader. All are priced at 25 cents.

60 THE DARK INVADER   *Captain von Rintelen*
Captain von Rintelen was the Kaiser's most dangerous saboteur and spy during World War I. The confessions which he makes in this book show how war-minded Germany seeks to demoralize the people and destroy the factories and shipping of her enemies. This book stands as a warning to Americans today.

79 THE RASP   *Philip MacDonald*
A completely worth-while mystery characterized by suspense, fast pace, smooth humor, and "scrupulously fair treatment of the reader."

239 STEALTHY TERROR   *John Ferguson*
Murder, suspense, pursuit, international intrigue, detection—this great thriller contains them all in large quantities.

276 THE CASE OF THE LATE PIG   *Margery Allingham*
An excellent mystery and a funny one, written by one of the foremost mystery authors of today.

339 HIGH RISING   *Angela Thirkell*
An extremely amusing novel by the author of *Marling Hall* and *The Brandons*. Mrs. Thirkell proves here, as never before, her ability to create sparkling conversation.

501 MURDER BY AN ARISTOCRAT   *Mignon G. Eberhart*
"Very ingeniously put together and, as usual with this author, the atmosphere of discomfort and suspense is well maintained." —*Dorothy L. Sayers.*

502 PYGMALION   *Bernard Shaw*
A handsomely illustrated edition of Shaw's famous play about
a London flower girl who, like Cinderella, is raised to the top of
the social ladder. The rest of the play, of course, has nothing to
do with the Cinderella myth.

503 DEATH OF A GHOST   *Margery Allingham*
One of today's most popular crime-story writers tells an excellent tale of the tortuous workings of a criminally insane mind.

504 ALL CONCERNED NOTIFIED   *Helen Reilly*
A good yarn that keeps you guessing. Miss Reilly plays fair
with the reader—perhaps fairer than any other famous mystery
author. An Inspector McKee story.

505 THE MOTHER   *Pearl S. Buck*
A great and unforgettable novel about family life in a village
in the interior of China. The Mother is one of the outstanding
characters of modern literature.

506 TWO SURVIVED   *Guy P. Jones*
A German surface raider sinks a merchantman in the South
Atlantic at night and attempts to annihilate the crew. But
under the cloak of darkness seven escape in a life boat. After
seventy days the boat is washed up on an island over 1,000
miles away, and the seven survivors have become only two. An
epic tale of the sea—and a true one!

507 THE PHYSIOLOGY OF SEX   *Kenneth Walker*
The facts of sex and the importance of sound sexual relation-
ships to the individual and the community.

508 WALDEN   *Henry David Thoreau*
One of the most amusing and most popular of the philosophical
works written during the period which marked what Van Wyck
Brooks rightly calls "The Flowering of New England." Illustrated
with wood cuts.

509 THE PASTURES OF HEAVEN   *John Steinbeck*
The author of *The Grapes of Wrath* at his best and most
charming. Every admirer of Steinbeck and every lover of good,
enjoyable writing will want to read this book.

510 TRENT'S OWN CASE   *E. C. Bentley and H. Warner Allen*
When murder strikes close to home, Philip Trent gives up a
resolve of long standing and works with the police on the
identification of the murderer. A classic among mysteries.

511 CAUSE FOR ALARM   *Eric Ambler*
A fast-paced spy story revealing the workings of an international munitions ring and the subtle but dangerous doings of
German, Russian, and Italian spies operating inside Italy. Includes one of the most hair-raising pursuits to be found anywhere.

512 THE STRANGE CASE OF MISS ANNIE SPRAGG   *Louis Bromfield*
An enjoyable and skillfully written novel by one of America's
most famous writers.

513 THE CATALYST CLUB   *George Dyer*
"This mystery novel is emphatically one of the good ones . . .
well-written, interesting, and really alive."
          —Kay Irwin in the *New York Times*

514 TOMBSTONE   *Walter Noble Burns*
The exciting, authoritative story of the old boom town of
Tombstone, Arizona, with its gamblers, Indian fighters, out-
laws, and two-gun sheriffs.

515 THE CONFIDENTIAL AGENT   *Graham Greene*
A spy story with a completely authentic background, written by
one of today's finest authors. Intrigues, counter-intrigues, and
plenty of action.

516 GENGHIS KHAN   *Harold Lamb*
The true story of Genghis Khan, Emperor of All Men, who was
without doubt the greatest conqueror the world has ever known.
The author is an authority on military history.

Penguin "Specials"

These important topical volumes are priced at the regular Penguin figure of 25 cents.

S75   NEW WAYS OF WAR   *Tom Wintringham*
The Second Edition of the famous book, first published in 1940, which has altered military thought more than any other work published in many years.

S82   AIRCRAFT RECOGNITION   *R. A. Saville-Sneath*
The most famous of all plane spotters' books. Silhouettes and descriptions of the 82 important British, German, and Italian aircraft, plus photos. A vocabulary of all terms used by airplane spotters. Revised and enlarged edition.

S201   WHAT'S THAT PLANE?   *Walter Pitkin, Jr.*
Silhouettes, photos, and descriptions of (1) American military and commercial planes; (2) Japanese military aircraft; and (3) German long-range military planes. Covers 83 planes in detail. Second edition, revised and enlarged.

S202   NEW SOLDIER'S HANDBOOK
The complete text of the official *Soldier's Handbook* as well as added material selected by *The Infantry Journal*.

S203   GUERRILLA WARFARE   *"Yank" Levy*
A prescription for all individuals and groups who may some time have to rely on guerrilla methods.

S204   HOW THE JAP ARMY FIGHTS   *Four U.S. Army Officers*
Military experts whose real business is fighting, not writing, describe the Japanese Army. Includes play-by-play descriptions of battles in China and Malaya. Illustrated.

S206   HOW RUSSIA PREPARED   *Maurice Edelman*
The Soviets' economic preparations for war. Emphasis is on the development of industry in the Urals.